FROM HELL on EARTH
To the
Foot of the Cross

AN AUTOBIOGRAPHY BY

Francine N. D'Aprile

Author of "Reflections into My Soul"

Order this book online at www.trafford.com
or email orders@trafford.com

Most Trafford titles are also available at major online book retailers.

Unless otherwise indicated, Scripture taken from the New King James Version.

Printed in the United States of America.

ISBN: 978-1-4269-6613-2 (sc)
ISBN: 978-1-4269-6614-9 (hc)
ISBN: 978-1-4269-6615-6 (e)

Library of Congress Control Number: 2011906439

Trafford rev. 09/07/2011

 www.trafford.com

North America & international
toll-free: 1 888 232 4444 (USA & Canada)
phone: 250 383 6864 ♦ fax: 812 355 4082

FROM HELL ON EARTH
TO THE
FOOT OF THE CROSS

AN AUTOBIOGRAPHY BY
FRANCINE N. D'APRILE
AUTHOR OF "REFLECTIONS INTO MY SOUL"

TABLE OF CONTENTS

I lovingly dedicate this book to my husband
Anthony G. D'Aprile

Tony once said,
"I would rather go back to Vietnam and fight
the enemy then be here and fight the thing
that was killing my wife."

This is my story.
This is a Modern Day Miracle.
This is the story of my husband's love for me
and his faith in God

ACKNOWLEDGMENT

This book would not have been possible without the encouragement of my husband, Tony, and my mother Elizabeth.

My husband has always been there for me. We have weathered many storms through our lives, but God has brought us through so that we could see the sunshine in the morning and the moon glowing at night.

My mother Elizabeth who passed away in 2003, always held me in her arms even when she was not with me. Through her personal relationship with God, He was there as she raised seven children by herself after the untimely death of my father James Tai Hook.

ABOUT THE AUTHOR

Francine Noelani Tai Hook was born in the city of Honolulu Oahu Hawaii, on February 23, 1949. She was raised in the city of Kaneohe on the windward side of the island, by a Christian Mother, with her 6 siblings, Melinda, Elizabeth, James, Wayne, Elsie, and Jerry. After graduation from Castle High School she traveled to Riverside, California. June 29, 1969 she married Anthony Gregory D'Aprile; after doing his tour of duty with the United States Marine Corp in South East Asia, Vietnam.

Because of her many health problems, Francine constantly was not able to do the many things she had set her life's goal on. Through Gods guiding hands and her husband's encouragement she decided to write this book on her struggles with Satan and his constant interference in her life. She tells of how a loving God was always there for her with His outstretched hands.

Francine has been blessed with two sons Wayne and Frank, a loving daughter in-law Michelle, four grandchildren Nikko, Nathan, Nalani, Nelissa, and a precious great grandson Caleb.

AUTHOR'S PREFACE

Those who write stories of their lives do so for specific reasons. Many authors write hoping that what they write about will inspire others. Some write for the love of writing, while others write out of sheer frustration. My story was written with the guidance of God through the Holy Spirit for a specific group of people.

From Hell on Earth to the Foot of the Cross, is written for those who feel they are living a life of *"hell on earth."* They have *"given up hope"* and have not seen *"The footprints on the sand."* It is written for those who say there is no black and there is no white! There is no right and there is no wrong! There is no good and there is no evil! There is no God and there is no devil! These people feel their life is void.

This book on the other hand is written for those who feel they are not living a life of *"hell on earth"* and have not *"given up hope"* and have seen the *"The footprints on the sand."* It is written for those who say there is black and there is white, there is right and there is wrong, there is good and there is evil, there is a God and there is a devil. Yet with all this they still feel their life is void.

Throughout my life I have been in both categories. I have seen and not seen what it is like to live a hell on earth, I have had hope in my life but I have also given up hope many times. I have seen and not seen the footprints on the sand. I have seen and not seen black and white. I have seen and not seen right and wrong. I have seen and not seen good and evil. I have seen and not seen God and the devil. Yet, my life was void and not void. For many years I wandered like a child lost in the wilderness.

Throughout my life, because of my Mother's faith and believe in God, I truly believe God does answer prayers, He perform miracles when the time is right and will perform miracles to those who least expect it. When God *"stretch forth His hand"* and spoke to me and told me to *"stretch forth thine hand"* I became a Fisher of Men, and now where He leads me I will follow. The journey will always be rough for those who reach out to Him.

As you read the story of my life and my conversion back into Christianity you will understand why it is a modern day miracle. You will read how the love and devotion of my husband kept me alive, and how his faith in God carried us through some very trying and difficult periods in our lives. Because my mind is constantly in the past I am still afraid of how people will judge me. Matthew 7:1-2 reads, "Judge not, that you be not judged. For with what judgment you judge, you will be judged; and with the measure you use, it will be measured back to you". I do not have to answer to anyone except my God, for He is the creator and the only one who will judge me.

For those who read my book, "may you always be blessed with God's grace and know that God is a real God, God is a forgiving God, God is a God of love and mercy, for He is my God! Because of His death on Calvary and His dying love for me I am closer to God when I am sitting at the foot of the cross. Because of His death on Calvary I can live to praise His name. Everyone has a chance for eternal life.

When I look at His nail pierced hands, I believe in a "Hill called Mt. Calvary", and when my life looks like there is no hope in this wicked world, I need only look up and know that He is there, and whatever I do be it good or bad He is still the Loving God that gave His life for me.

Yours in Christ, Francine Noelani D'Aprile

CHAPTER ONE
THE ALPHA - PARADISE

"Train up a child in the way he should go,
and when he is old he will not depart from it".
Proverbs 22:6

My name is Francine Noelani Tai Hook D'Aprile and I am a native Hawaiian, not because I was born in Hawaii but because that is my heritage and my bloodline. I was born in "paradise" on the island of Oahu, on February 23, 1949, to Elizabeth Lizzie Kahalekai Kelii-kuhalahala Tai Hook and James Hulihonua Tai Hook.

Oahu known as The Gathering Place is the third largest of the Hawaiian Islands. During the time of my birth it was called the Territory of Hawaii. Hawaii did not become a state until August 21, 1959. The Hawaiian Island chain comprises of hundreds of island but the main eight islands are knows as Ni'ihau, Kaua'i, O'ahu, Moloka'i, Lana'i, Kaho'olawe, Maui and Hawai'i. The island of Hawai'i is usually known as the Big Island to avoid confusion with the state as a whole.

Let me paint you a picture of my childhood days. I was brought up in what people call "paradise", and spent my childhood and teen years in the city of Kaneohe; meaning "bamboo man", in the District of Koolaupoko. During my childhood days and later into my teens, Kaneohe, had a very beautiful appearance, its low land and valley at one time was crowded with plantations of taro, sugarcane and sweet potatoes. Mango, macadamia nuts, papaya and other tropical fruit trees could be found all over my little town.

The flowers that bloomed everywhere gave the town the scent of white gardenias, purple orchids, yellow plummeries and red gingers, to name a few. From my mother's house you could see the Ko'olau Mountain range in all its beauty and splendor. It is not a mountain range in the normal sense, because it was formed as a single mountain called Ko'olau Volcano. The word ko'olau means "windward" in Hawaiian. On rainy days you can see hundreds of waterfalls, cascading down the mountain, then disappearing into the green luscious forest giving each plant and tree the gift of life. It is so awesome to look at it.

Hawaii in the 1940's was turbulent years, December 7, 1941, just before 8am Sunday morning is forever to be remembered in World History; the bombing of Pearl Harbor. It would bring great sadness and great sorrow to the people of Hawaii. As I grew up and studied about Pearl Harbor I could not help but feel like my little island had been raped; stripped of its dignity. In the end no one won, just memories of lives lost and the beauty of the island scarred forever.

Martial Law in Hawaii ended in 1944. The Hawaiian citizens were given their legal rights back, and on August 14, 1945, news came to the islands that Japan had surrendered to the United States. The loss that Hawaii took would be devastating. The loss that the island people took is unimaginable. There are still painful memories in those who lived it, the stories that were told to their children and grandchildren. I was one of those children whose mother lived through that period in time.

On the island of Oahu, the most famous memorial to the bombing of Pearl Harbor is the ship "USS Arizona". The USS Arizona is the final resting place for the crewmen who lost their lives on December 7, 1941. The memorial structure spans the mid-portion of the sunken battle ship. Although a suggestion for a memorial began in 1943, it wasn't until 1949, when the Territory of Hawaii established the Pacific War Memorial Commission; the first real steps were taken to bring it about.

The USS Arizona Memorial was completed on May 25, 1962, but would not be dedicated till a few days later on Memorial Day. This Memorial would embody the tragedy of a nation. This Memorial would be a place where Americans and those who would come to the island to visit could come to mourn an event that was far beyond anyone's comprehension.

On April 1, 1946, Hawaii was hit by a huge tidal wave which claimed the lives of over a hundred people. There was a warning going out to everyone and people understood what was happening but since it was April Fools ' Day, some people ignored the warnings. It was also in this year that the Hawaii Visitors Bureau began to promote Hawaii on the mainland and abroad. Hawaii was still a territory and it would be another ten years after my birth before Hawaii would become the 50th state.

This was my Hawaii, this was my Island of Love, this was The Land of My Birth, and this is where the journey of my lifetime would begin. Like an artist that chooses the many different colors to paint a picture, and the various brushes used to make a picture painting come to life, my past will unfold like a bud before its blooming flower, like a tapestry sewn together piece by piece on my journey through life. As the needle pulls its white thread to join the pieces together, the thread will turn colors as each piece is joined together to tell about the different phases of my life.

Happily I was born into a family of love, the youngest of seven children, a most favored position in the family tree to receive lots of affection and attention. Hawaii was paradise as far as I was concerned. But, my Endenic Garden in the Pacific would be shattered at the age of three. My father died and left my sweet Christian mother alone in the struggle to raise seven children. Fortunately, Mama's life was centered on God as her guide and the blessed hope of the Seventh Day Adventist Church. My mother gave all seven of her children a good Christian upbringing.

I am grateful, now that early on she taught me that the Bible is a sacred and holy book. She told me when you read the Bible you will know where you came from, how to live your life and where I would go. The Bible was to be used as a guide book and that God will always be there for me. She said, "Noe in times of trouble, God is only a prayer away".

As the youngest child I didn't have to do much, and when I did anything, it was always a game to me. I used to spend hours counting the different trees, flowers, or bushes in my "Garden of Eden".

My earliest recollections were days spent picking macadamia nuts off the ground, counting the plumeria trees; buds and flowers, and spending more hours climbing the mango trees. Then if I got hungry and was too lazy to make me something to eat, I would find a hammer and crack the hard-shelled macadamia nut that I had gathered; hoping that when I hit it, I wouldn't miss and the nut would go flying in the air and hitting something. If I was lucky and the meat from the nut was ready, it would come out perfect, if not I would have to dig the nut meat out to get what I wanted. Usually the sweetness from the macadamia satisfied my need for sugar.

If it wasn't sweet enough to my satisfaction I would go hunting around the garden looking for sugarcane that my mom grew. Finding the stalks I would pull it down till I could break it off then remove the rind so that I could get into the internal part of the sugarcane to suck out its sweet juice or munch on it. I don't ever remember chewing on sugarcane that was not sweet.

Next to the sugarcanes there were more mango trees, so I would climb up a mango tree once again and find me a ripe firm mango and bite off the skin and eat the rest of the mango. If the mango was sweet and juicy it was difficult to eat because the mango was wet and its juice would be dripping and it felt like it would slip off between your fingers and onto the ground. Of course finding and eating the fruits made it so much easier and enjoyable then making me a sandwich. If I got energetic enough, I would find mangos that were half ripe, than I would cut the skin off and slice the meat into pieces and put it in a mixture of soy sauce, sugar, and salt.

My grandmother, Annie Kupuna Akaka Kelii-kuhalahala or Tutu-mama, was the Matriarch of the Ohana (family) and so we had a constant stream of relatives coming over. My grandfather, Daniel Kelii-kuhalahala or Tutu-papa had passed away a year before I was born.

I was always interested when the History of Hawaii or the family genealogy was brought into the conversation. I would run out of the house to play hide and go seek with my cousins, but would always return in plenty of time to sit at the foot of one of my elders and hear what they had to say. To me it was a privilege to hear stories first hand by those who had lived and experience old Hawaii and its traditions. The traditions were getting lost in the new generation and I wanted so much to keep it the way it was, never letting it go and always remembering happy times in the days of my youth.

Changes have never been easy for me. When you have a simple life and new things are introduced everything seems to get cluttered and lost and soon what was once a simple life becomes complicated by everything that is presented before you.

I was taught by my Tutus brother, my beloved Tutu Kamaka to value the Hawaiian culture, to discipline yourself to learn what you can even if no one is around to teach you, but to learn by doing. Sometimes people don't appreciate the beauty of something until they don't have it. My Tutu Kamaka would make these Hawaiian flower leis; the flowers were called Kukuna-o-ka-la. I loved the color of the flower because it reminded me of the rays of the sun, yellow, orange and red. The top of each flower was sharp and when you got poked it really hurt. Tutu Kamaka would string the flowers and made leis; a garland to wear, and would give it to me with love. I had always considered him my grandpa.

It was not until so many years had passed did I find the true meaning of him giving me this flower lei. In the summer he would go in the streams in brackish water having to fight off the mosquitoes and sloshed knee deep in swamp mud and water then come home and sew a lei and give it to me. There was so much love in the leis that he gave me. It was leis of "aloha" it was leis of "love". Below is a picture of my Tutu Kamaka, till today I still miss him a lot and think of him often.

Here is a picture of my tutu Kamaka who was loved by everyone. Till today I still miss him a lot and think of him often when I am singing.

Having no father I hung on to him as if he was I mean he wasn't even my grandfather, he was my grandmother's brother and yet I called him my grandfather. He lived on the land where we lived. He was always there. He always sang to me and would play the ukulele. I think that is why I loved playing the ukulele and singing so much, because there was so much love and happiness when it was sung to me when I was young.

During this phase in my life I learned about respect (ho'ihi). As with my Hawaiian ancestors before me I learned and understood the importance of treating each person with respect. At an early age I watched my grandmother and then my mother run the family household with love toward their children and other family members and learned that I must live that way throughout my life. This was part of the Hawaiian culture, to have and live the Aloha (love) spirit.

While my grandmother was alive, she took a trip to California. On her return she told us of all the different things she had seen and what she had bought. The stories she told me of California intrigued me; you have to remember at the time I had never left the island, I was just a young island girl. The day after my Grandmother came back from California I found the biggest and tallest mango tree that I could climb. When I finally got to the top of the mango tree, I sat on one of the many branches that would hold me and pushed the leaves and mangoes away from my face. There in my own little world I would try to imagine what California was like.

I had never been in a plane or left the islands let alone the city that I lived in. To me California seemed an eternity away and I could not imagine what that strange faraway place was like. For all I knew. my grandmother had gone to the mainland and she had enjoyed herself.

My imagination would get carried away and I thought I could fly. Within a few seconds reality would sink in and I realized I could not fly from the top of the mango tree or any other tree at any time. Scrambling down the tree just like a monkey I would jump to the ground with my bare feet and hit the dirt hard. Losing balance and almost falling flat on my face, I would straighten up and continue playing in the yard.

At the end of my family's property, I would continue on to my next destination. On the other side of the dirt road was a church. The church was not fenced in, the lawn was always cut so nice and the grass always looked so soft and welcoming. When no one was around I would slip into the church property and would lie on the grass and look up into the skies.

As far as I can remember, Hawaii always had the most beautiful blue skies, and when the clouds rolled by they looked like cotton candy. When I stared up into the sky, the clouds would be moving so fast and I was fascinated by its speed. Occasionally a nice cool trade wind would pass over me and the sun was warm enough and bright enough to give me a nice Hawaiian tan.

On this particular day I thought of faraway places and my mom. My faraway places would be what I dreamed about; France, Switzerland, Italy, etc. I use to play the piano and sing the song "Far Away Places" for my mom, and the words "going to China" reminded me of my Mom because she had always wanted to go to China. A couple years before my Mom passed away in 2003 her dream would come true when she went on a vacation to China with her friends.

As I continued daydreaming in this peaceful spot, I wondered what California would be like. On other days when I was on the church property, as I looked up into the sky a bird or two would go gliding by or I would see a plane flying past my way. A helicopter would whiz by at times. My house was located across the Kaneohe Bay from the Kaneohe Marine Corps Base; little did I know that one day I would meet my future husband from the same base.

After spending what seemed like hours on a lazy Hawaiian day, I would walk across the road to the cemetery where my Dad and other family members were buried. Those were days when I would just sit and talk to my Dad telling him where I had been and what I had done. Of course at the cemetery it was always a one sided conversation. I would do the same to my other relatives and talk to them. To me it was like telling someone a secret and no one else would know, and no one else would tell. At times I would straighten up the flowers, or flower leis that others had left.

On Memorial Day, or other holidays, the cemetery would come alive with colors from every flower, flower leis, wreaths, etc. that you could think of. But there was nothing more beautiful than during the Christmas and Easter season. The red of the Poinsettias and the whites of the Lilly of the Valley would be seen all over the cemetery. At times a relative or friends would drive by and wave to me, or stop to see what I was doing. People that I didn't know would stop and talk to me. It was a time when living in Hawaii was so simple, so easy, so forgiving of everything.

When I wasn't sitting and talking to my dead relatives I would be running from headstone to headstone trying to read the names and dates on each one. As young as I was I would calculate in my head how old these people were, when they died, and wondered how and why. Sometimes there would be pictures, and I couldn't even imagine that person was under the ground.

The cemetery was my playground and everyone was asleep as far as I was concerned. I had to pass the cemetery everyday no matter where I was going; it was right across the road from where we lived. It didn't bother me at all to be there. Through my study of the bible I knew that the dead know not I was so young and didn't get the full conception of the bible text but at that time frame, the cemetery was just one big playground for me. "They are dead, they will not live; they are deceased, they will not rise. Therefore you have punished and destroyed them and made all their memory to perish." Isaiah 26:14

My mother became a widow at an early age; I was only three at the time. She was left to raise seven children by herself. I have no true recollection of my father, just what my mother has told me about him and whatever research I could find on him.

Even though I would go to the cemetery I didn't really know who this man was, but in my heart and as an innocent child I wanted so much to know the man I never knew, the father who I wanted so much. I was his secret admirer. Yes he had left us and died, and my heart would ache because I wanted to be like the other kids and have a Daddy with me all the time. Maybe if he was there my Mom wouldn't have had to work so hard. When he passed away I had my three older brothers take his place, and three older sisters to be there with me when my Mom was working and I knew that no matter what, I would have my brothers and sisters as friends. So I was truly blessed.

It would be a long time before I would realize that a child's fantasy was just that, a child's fantasy. I wanted so much to have a Daddy like other kids, and my Mom to have a husband to help raise my brothers, sisters and me. I wanted so much to have a father that I talked to a dead man who could not hear me, talk to me, see me, or even be with me. My mother must have had such sadness when my dad died, and such concern knowing she had so much to take care of all of us. How she must have grieved over the years, but she had so much love because of her faith in God.

July 5, 1960 my Grandmother, Annie Kupuna Kelii-kuhalahala died. My Grandmother had been such a kind and loving person. To use the words "had been" was hard to swallow. Grandma (Tutu) had a soft sweet voice; she had done so much for so many. Now she was gone, my beloved Tutu. No more would I see her smile, her beautiful white hair, and most important of all her warmth and loving hugs.

The day of her funeral there were so many people, so many cars. Everything that was going on that day I hated; only because I couldn't truly understand what was going on. This was the first funeral that I remembered going to. My Mom had bought me a beautiful white dress and new shoes but I did not want to wear the dress or put on the shoes.

When I entered the funeral parlor and made my way up to my Tutu's coffin, I was crying and trembling, holding on to my mother. Inside I was shaking like a leaf, I was a kid then and death had finally come into my household. This was our final good-byes to the woman that gave so much. I looked around and there were so many flowers. I hadn't seen so many wreaths in all my life, so many bouquets, so many pots of plants at one time, so many flower leis. My Tutu was in the flower lei business. On this day there was no beauty in the flowers. All the flowers to me had the scent of death, the smell of death. To me the floral arrangements were lifeless, like the lifeless body I was about to encounter.

Finally I reached my Tutu's coffin, it was the longest walk I had or would ever take. Now as I step forward to look at my Tutu, she laid there in that box, so quiet, so still, her hands cross and folded. In my young mind I kept thinking, "get up, get up, get up". Say something, smile, why are you so quiet? You are not smiling, why? I can see you, can't you see me, and can't you say something? Make these people stop crying, please. It was too much for a kid to take in.

I looked around me and saw so many people there to bid my grandmother farewell; family, so many friends and acquaintances that would miss her so much.

My Grandmother, like my Mother was a great influence in my life. Grandmother's profile was that of a woman who was gentle in words, kind in heart, and her smile would light up a room when she walked in. When my grandmother died, the gentleness, the kindness the lights went out for so many people. Now I stood next to her coffin, this horrible box, starring at her, it was the most horrible feeling an 11 year old could have had or wanted. Mom told me to kiss Grandma, but I didn't want to, I didn't know what to expect. The fear of the unknown can cause so many emotions. It brings emotions that you didn't even know you had.

My mother kept telling me to kiss my Grandmother, but I did not want to, I hated it, and who was this person laying in this box, in this coffin. I had no choice and so I bent over to kiss her with tears gushing down my face. I was horrified at the coldness that I felt coming from her, like cement that is hard. All of a sudden I knew what death was all about. It was looking at me right in the face. Suddenly I could feel the sorrow, the pain, the grief, the sadness and loneliness that only a child could feel given the situation. I felt I had been forced to kiss something that was foreign to me.

My emotions were confused, I couldn't see the strained look with tears streaming down everyone's face like someone had opened a water faucet and forgot to turn it off. It just came gushing. The blank look on every ones face, like it can't be happening. The Matriarch of the family forever silenced.

This was not my Grandma, how could she be my grandmother? This person that I had just kissed whose face was as cold as cement, no smile, no laughter, no warmth, no love, no movement, no sound, no heartbeat, just silence. In the midst of the storm there was just silence. For my Grandma, my Tutu, the music had stopped, no life, a cold body, death, curtain close only a name that would be mentioned in passing when relatives got together and then eventually would be forgotten, but I didn't want anyone to forget my Grandma, my Tutu.

Days, weeks and months after her death, I would cry myself to sleep. When I looked at the ilima flowers my Grandmother's flower, the beauty was still there but the life of the flower was missing from it. The red gingers, red anthurians, white gardenias, yellow plumeria, seem lifeless. Something was now missing. When it would rain, I would look at the statuous Koolau Mountain Range with its hundreds of waterfalls cascading down to nowhere, to me they were now crying just like I was. Like the waterfalls cascading down to nowhere, so were my tears, not knowing where to go.

The morning they buried my Grandmother there was such sadness, the funeral procession slowly made its way from the mortuary to the cemetery. Now as we all gathered to say our last goodbyes, and sing the song "Face to Face", her coffin slowly was lowered to the ground. As the workers lowered her coffin inch by inch, it was like a stab in the heart, inch by inch. When it finally was lowered all the way to the bottom of the hole, you could hear the silent crying and sniffling, and then the realization that her life was truly over.

As the days, weeks, months and years went by, whenever I went to the cemetery I would completely block out the scene of the funeral parlor and what happened that day. The cemetery was still one of my playing grounds and I continued to go there. Being alone was golden, no one telling me what to do. I would not let myself connect the funeral parlor scene with the cemetery. At the mortuary Grandma was dead; at the cemetery she was asleep.

My Grandmother Annie Kupuna Kelii-kuhalahala.

After I left Hawaii, for years every time I went back to visit my family and friends, I would take a walk by myself to my old playing ground, the cemetery. Sometimes I took flowers or leis. Going by myself I would sit alone in silence, my mind would reflect back to my childhood days. It was still the same place, but now, having a better understanding of death, I was not drawn to continue going there.

Eventually I stopped going, and would not go back to the cemetery until my grand-daughter Nalani and I visited Hawaii. After that, it would be years that I would visit the cemetery until I went back in 2003 to say good bye to my Mom. That would be the hardest day of my life because now I truly knew how my Mom felt and how she missed her Mom till the day she died. When my mother died it would be my turn to tell my Mother goodbye and how I miss her so much. But I will see her in heaven and we will sing Gods praises together.

My beloved mother, Elizabeth Kahalekai Kelii-kuhalahala Tai Hook.

On one of my visits to Hawaii, I took my grand-daughter Nalani with me for a visit. I took her to her great, grandfather's grave site. I told her what I knew about him. The headstone that was once bigger than life to me was just a small insignificant piece of worn out cement. As Nalani sat next to the headstone, I couldn't help but think I was that little when my Dad died. In my heart I told my Daddy goodbye and thanked him for keeping me company and listening to my little secrets and hopes for the future when we were there alone by ourselves. I thanked him for giving me three older brothers to take his place; I thanked him for giving me three older sisters, and I thanked him for giving Mom us seven kids, to fill the void that she would have when he died.

Now the little girl that once roamed the cemetery, that once talked to the dead, that once poured her little heart out, that once ached in her heart for this dead father to come alive, had grown up. Those years for me will always hold a special place in my heart. As I walked away from his gravesite I turned around once more and looked back and there I saw myself as a little girl smiling and waving goodbye and then I heard a little voice calling, "Grandma" my grand-daughter Nalani was smiling and sitting by my Dad's headstone. The past was in back of me, and my precious grand-daughter was the future looking in front of me.

My grand-daughter Nalani sitting next to her
Great Grandpas headstone.

In March 2009, I had a book of poems published. The title of the book was called "Reflections into My Soul". One of the poems that I wrote was about my Dad and my three older brothers, James, Wayne, and Jerry. Although we all live apart, James in Hawaii, Wayne in Canada, Jerry in Las Vegas, and me in California, in our hearts we will always be together till the day we die. When I look up in the sky, I always think of my brothers and sisters and in my heart I would silently say "if you're out their looking too, I'm sending my love to you".

This poem is dedicated to my brothers James, Wayne and Jerry.

"The Man I Never Knew"
By Francine N. D'Aprile © 2009

I wish I knew My Dad the Man I never met, because He left me at three His time on earth had long been set. Except for pictures that I have and few words my Mom would say, my Dad is the Man I never knew but I learned about Him along life's way. When I look at my Brothers in each and every one of them I see, a little something about the Man I never knew looking back at me.

When my Brothers speak, is that the voice of the Man I never knew? And when I glance at their eyes I wonder what they view? I sing along with my Brothers we laugh, we sit and talk, are they fulfilling the part of the Man I never knew are they fulfilling His walk? Many a time in the lonely hours when darkness never seems to end, the Man I never knew actually became my friend. No matter what the situation, depending on the day, the Man I never knew always seemed to be in my way.

I've pondered and wondered year after year to search for something I would never find, it bothered me constantly it was always on my mind. How could I be so dumb to search for something that I knew did not exist? But like a child who doesn't know any better, it was my greatest wish.

The Man I never knew is the Dad I never had, but it really doesn't matter, you see life hasn't been so bad. After all these years I've stopped wondering about the Man I never knew, a long time ago God gave me three older Brothers and that is quite a few.

When people talk about their Dads, and the holidays that have passed, I am so lucky to talk about my three older Brothers whose memories are a mass. So the Dad I never knew, I thank Him with all my heart, because He gave me three older brothers and in our hearts we are never apart.

My Dad, James Tai Hook, taken March 26, 1947
at Agana Hill Air field in Guam.

Continuing my story when I was growing up in Hawaii, my years in grade school would be happy ones except when I reached the third grade. For some reason I developed a speech impediment and I could not pronounce my S's. So instead of saying; Saturday, I would say taturday, instead of saying Sunday I would say tunday and so it went on and on. I had to go to a "special class"; I hated to go to it because kids made fun of you when you had to be in these "special class".

Here I am in the picture above, eight years old in the special education class. Some kids called it the "dummies" class. Being only eight it was really hard and it made it worse when kids in school started to tease me and make fun of the way I talked. I felt like an outsider not belonging in any of my classes or at the school, I couldn't understand why kids would be so mean. They would tease me; you talk funny, you talk funny and for a third grader it was not easy, and when they laugh at me I just wanted to dig a hole and bury myself.

Now I hated school and no matter how much I would laugh and smile, inside I would cry to myself and couldn't understand why I was being taunted. I had always been sheltered within my family because of so many of us and being the youngest. My only salvation was now my family. After all, who needs a bunch of kids making fun of me? I didn't need anyone. I had my brothers and sisters to play with. I could always run to my Mom when I needed a hug.

The Special Speech class that I now had to go to and how I was treated was to be my first encounter with what the real world was like. I hated the kids who teased me at the time because of my speech impediment. I think it was then that I started to learn that unless you walk in someone else's shoe then just be a friend no matter what.

What might seem small in our eyes, to the person that has to bear that cross, it is a heavy cross to bear no matter how little. But God has a way of seeing things way ahead of time and this little incident would make me understand why I was allowed to have this happen to me. This small little insignificant thing would leave such an impression on me, and from that day forward I would never make fun of those who are disabled mentally or physically because I have not walked in their shoes. I often think of that year when I had to go to that "special class" where I had to work so hard to pronounce my S's, the way they should be, but the cruelty that was thrust upon me at that time, would last me a life time.

Coming from a family with seven kids and being the youngest made it a special place for me. I have always appreciated my family then as I do now. My brothers James, Wayne, Jerry, and my sisters Melinda, Elizabeth, and Elsie have always held a very special place in my heart. In each one of my siblings I see my Dad and Mom. Not so much my Dad, but so much my Mom. It might be the way they talked or the way they waked or just a gesture they made. Of course as the years have gone by, our family of seven has continued to grow, with in-laws, nieces and nephews, with over a hundred and still growing.

As I once talked to my Uncles and Aunties over 50 years ago, I find myself in their position as my nieces and nephews ask me questions about family history. I can now talk to them about our Ohana, our beloved family and how important they are to us.

When I was in the 6th grade I was transferred to a private church school. This would be a whole new experience for me. It was different and since I made friends pretty easily transferring to a different school was no problem. I loved the school, and the whole atmosphere centered on Jesus. Coming from a family with the same religious practice at the new school I attended made it very easy for me to fit into this new found school.

The school was a Seventh Day Adventist Mission school, it was very small and I was in a class room with kids from three grades, 6th, 7th and 8th. My 6th grade class consisted of 15 boys and 4 girls and they would be my classmates for the next three years.

When I was in the seventh grade I was given the opportunity to take piano lessons. Financially it would be a hardship on my mom, but she knew how badly I wanted to take piano lessons. It was $2.00 for 30 minutes. After school every Tuesday, I would take a 15-20 minute walk from the school to get to the house where I was taking private lessons. The walk was always nice, at that time I attended a school in the city of Kailua, not Kaneohe, and since the school was pretty close to the beach, I could feel the nice breeze hitting my face.

I can still see my piano teacher's face. She was very strict. I think she was in her 60's and she reminded me of a Drill Sergeant. What and how she taught me would be something that again would carry me through life. She said, "You cannot just play the piano you have to want to play it, you have to have a passion for it and you must want to practice, practice, practice and you must always be patient with yourself".

After that came the Drill Sergeant. If I hit the wrong note she would hit my hands with a stick not hard but enough to know I better get it right, and then she would drill into my head, you must Practice! Practice! Practice! "She said you must be disciplined in your practicing. I took lessons for about a year and then I couldn't take anymore because my Mom just couldn't afford it.

During those three years at this private Mission School, I had so much fun. There were times when I caught the church bus. I couldn't wait to get to school and when I went home I couldn't wait to get on the phone so I could talk to my best friend about the boys. Well before I knew it the three years had passed by and eighth grade graduation was here. Our color theme was blue and our flowers were Vanda Orchids.

After the graduation ceremony was over, we went to the home of one of our classmates; his dad was a doctor and they had a huge house with a swimming pool. We all said our goodbyes knowing we probably would never see anyone again. To me they would become like strangers passing through the night; I hope if any of my classmates read this book they will see the connection and contact me.

Since graduating from the Eighth grade class, I have only met one of my classmates who went to the same high school as me, but it would be 40 years later at a class reunion. He now lives in Japan and has a performing arts school. The memories I have of those childhood days are memories of a time and place when God was truly guiding me.

Music had become a very important part of my life and I made sure I took every music class that I could take ans that was offered me in high school. During these years and prior years, I was very involved with the church and played the piano, sang in the choir, sang solos, and helped in the Sabbath School class rooms.

I joined our high school choir, took piano classes, and got involved with anything that had to do with music also. At home I did what I had done years before: practice, practice, practice playing the piano. As the years went by I also learned so many different crafts. Because money was tight when I was growing up, I learned to do a lot of things on my own to keep me occupied. At this point in my life, God was my constant guide. He was always just a prayer and a song away from me.

Times were changing and most of my siblings, if not all were out of the house. I got to spend a lot of precious time with my mother. Like all teenagers, it was a growing time, a time for decisions. I was not a child running around barefooted in t-shirts and shorts anymore. At 17 I wanted to do more then what I was doing. I had met a Marine that I was interested in, but he was on his way to Vietnam.

Vietnam I didn't know too much about it at the time, except it was where my boyfriend and two of my brothers were going. The war in Vietnam was getting bad and I wondered when it would end I knew that there were guys in my high school that were worried about going over there once they got drafted. Later I would find out that one of my classmates went there and not too long after being in Vietnam he was killed; so young, only 18. It seemed that a country so far away would one day be so much a part of my life.

Now that I would be graduating, I hadn't really thought about what I was going to do after graduation. In fact now when I think about it, I had no future plans in mind.

During my high school years my oldest sister Melinda (Omi) and her husband Eddie moved to California, so for graduation they sent me a plane ticket to come visit them. I talked to my mom about it. She wasn't too happy because she didn't want me to leave since I had spent so much time with her and was the only one home with her. But I had decided that after graduation I wanted more than just living in Hawaii. I wanted to get away from my tiny little island. I decided I would not only visit my sister but would at the same time move there to live.

June 10, 1967, I graduated from James B. Castle High School, Kaneohe, Hawaii. During the ceremony I would cry knowing three or four days later I would board the plane for California and would leave behind a lifetime of memories. I would leave my family, friends, church and home. Everything that had been a part of my life for the first 18 years of my life would now disappear behind me.

The first chapter in my life had ended, my childhood days gone and now the days of my youth just about over, what was in store I had no idea. Another phase of my life would begin but now it would take place in a different state. The picture that God had painted for the first 18 years of my life had been completed. There were still many phases of my life that were not put on the canvas, those memories would forever be locked away in my mind.

Now sitting by myself in the plane, I leaned back and thought of the days when I used to look up into the sky and could only wonder and dream what it would be like to fly in a plane. As the tears slowly started to roll down my face, my island that I had so loved, the land of my birth, my ohana (family) waving goodbye, the simple life that I had once known slowly faded away, like the islands below me diminishing into nowhere.

I was in the clouds closer to God then I had ever been before. He was the artist that held the brush in His hands. He had the palette of many colors to choose from. He would paint the rest of my life for me. Up in the skies among the clouds God would always be with me and I knew why my mother always put Him first in her life. I knew even though I would move on, what had been instilled in me during my childhood days would never leave me.

I knew what my Mom had taught me about God would never leave my side. I knew now why she had loved the Lord He had been good to her in all her struggles in life.

A new phase of my life was about to begin. My life in Hawaii had now ended. I now had a clean paint brush, an empty canvas and a palette full of paint. What would God put in my life to paint next?

CHAPTER TWO
A TIME FOR EVERY THING

"To everything there is a season, and a time to every purpose under the heaven". Ecclesiastes 3:1

The reason I called this chapter "A Time for Every Thing" is because from here on "everything" that affected my life would be my responsibility; God would hand the paint brush, canvas, and paint to me. I was now 18 and had graduated from high school. My mother wouldn't be there to hold my hand. What I had learned early in life was instilled in me. The days of my youth would forever be embedded in my mind. I would now make the call be it good or bad, whatever choices or decisions that I made were something that I would have to live with. Now "everything" that I did in my life would have a purpose. At the end of the day and at the bottom of my life line, my signature would be there.

It was June 1967 when I went to California. It was the first time I was going to ride a plane and go to another state, but not only going to another state, but crossing the Pacific Ocean. I didn't know what to expect, what would happen if the plane just fell out of the sky? It is funny what goes through a persons' mind when they are going into the unknown and this was truly unknown for me.

I was amazed that here I was finally on a plane going to some destination that was called California. I would see my sister who I had not seen for a while. I really missed her and had always looked up to her. She had always been kind to me like my other two sisters and she had always pushed herself to get ahead. All I remember was that she was always working, always keeping busy. I was excited, but I could still picture my Mom's face, tears running down her checks and not wanting to let me go, her hug so tight. The plane finally hit the runway, the sound so loud you wonder what is going to happen next. Minutes later the plane came to a complete stop.

The Stewardess got up and welcomed everyone to California and then added on other instructions and where to go. I was ready to get out of the plane since I felt cramped on the plane, I didn't know what to expect. As I got out of the plane and walked the short hallway into the airport, the air and everything else seemed so different. This was not Hawaii, the air was hot and to me there seemed to be hundreds of people. There was so much hustle and bustle, I longed for my family in Hawaii and the smiles that I no longer saw. I didn't know anyone and felt so all alone. Finally I saw my sister Melinda and brother in-law Eddie waiting for me, and I was so happy to see familiar faces.

The drive back to Riverside seemed endless. I had never been on a freeway and passed so many cities, cars, trucks, vehicles all zipping by like ants. I was amazed at the sight of so many high buildings. When we finally got to Riverside it now seemed hotter than ever and I wondered if I had made the right decision to leave Hawaii. The heat was different and there was no island breeze. Living in California would be a challenge for me. The people, the food, the atmosphere, everything different then what I was used to.

My sister lived in the city of La Sierra, Riverside County, California, and worked at the Adventist College within that city and a couple of days after things were settled, my sister took me on a tour of the college I would be attending, the city of Riverside and its other surrounding cities. The most amazing thing to me at that time was all the orange trees. I had never seen an orange tree. Mango tree, yeah, guava tree, yeah, papaya tree, yeah, orange tree, no. Because of the heat I couldn't wait to get back to her house. Of course she had an air conditioner, but living in Hawaii you got the trade winds.

That night I couldn't wait to call my mom up and tell her what I had seen and done but by the end of the night I was out. The next morning I got up and opened my curtains and everything was white, I asked my sister what was happening and she explained to me about fog. I had never see fog before I began to feel more and more like I was in a strange land and not in the United States.

Well you can say for the next year there were a lot of firsts for me, especially the food. The food was different. What were tacos? What were tostadas? When we went to the store they didn't have the things I was used to eating. Where was the poi, and fish? There would be a lot of adjustments to make. All I knew was that I was in California, there were so many cars and freeways and life was going to be different. Could I truly adjust to everything?

It was summer time and I was lucky to have a sister that worked at the college. She helped me get a job and I told her I would take anything just so that I could have some spending money. The first job that was offered was at the college where my sister worked. It was at their in house Laundromat I also did janitorial work during the week. On Sundays I worked at the college egg farm. Not only was I making extra money but it gave me an opportunity to find my way around the college campus. I cannot help but laugh at all the experiences that I went through.

I laugh when I think of one incident at the college egg farm. I used to sit and pull the bad eggs that I found that came off of this conveyor belt on the machine that I was working on. You would look through a light and if you saw any discoloration or something weird you pulled the egg off of the conveyor belt. It was a lot of fun, but I think everything was fun to me because I lived in a simple world in my mind, and was fascinated by everything.

This particular day my boss came in. My boss was from some European country and he had the neatest accent. His daughter also worked with us and sometimes they would talk in their native language. He was a big hearty man and treated all his employees fairly. He told me that he wanted me to go outside and learn some of the other jobs and asked if I would be interested I said sure. After all, I was always on the outside when I lived in Hawaii and to work in a building, I would have given anything to go outside.

My first job would be to drive the carts with the eggs on it. Well the eggs were put on flat cartons and stacked on top of each other so that it was maybe 3 or 4 feet high. The cart was hooked on a driving contraption. There were hundreds of eggs on this cart. When I was taught how to drive this cart, it seemed so easy, I think even the chickens could have driven it. It was also a lot of fun, but at the time there were no eggs on the back of the cart.

I was having so much fun collecting the eggs, stacking it on the cart and driving it to wherever I had to take it. At this time there must have been at least 1 or 2 hundred flat cartons full with eggs. I was so caught up in the fun of driving this egg cart I wasn't paying attention to where I was going. As I made the turn to go to where I was supposed to make the turn, I did not realize how fast I had turned. As I looked in the back of the cart to make the turn, in slow motion I started to see egg cartons slide off the cart, and then the eggs started slowly rolling, and rolling and rolling and then there were cracked eggs all over the place. I couldn't believe my eyes, needless to say that was my last duty as an egg cart driver. Thank goodness my boss was so good to me and just took it in stride and told me it was back to the egg house for me, where I could look at them and not break them.

I started college in the fall. Of course my major was music; when I was in my senior year of high school, I had been offered a music scholarship, but at the time college was not on my mind, so I declined. Now I wish I had taken the scholarship.

The first year in California I had the better of two worlds as far as school living conditions were concerned. I did not live on campus so I did not have the restriction of campus life. I did have friends from Hawaii living in the dormitory so when I visited them I got to see what living on campus was like. Because my sister was affiliated with the college, I got to live with her and I loved living with my oldest sister and her husband. My sister and her husband bought a piano just for me and spoiled me silly. On many weekends we drove to Oxnard in their little Volks Wagon and spent the weekends with my Aunty and her family. Those were fun times, times of memories, once again, when life was so simple.

On the other weekends my sister would invite students from Hawaii that lived in the dormitory over to her house to eat and socialize. It was nice being with the "local" people of Hawaii. I couldn't have asked for a better place to live at the time. I will always be grateful and thankful for the time I spent with my sister and her husband in the early years of my adult life. I would truly know what it was to be blessed with a Christian family.

Well I got registered for college and once the semester began I was so excited about attending the classes. The atmosphere in school was so different then what I had known. Because of the way I talked; using English mixed with pigeon English and that Hawaiian slang, I had to take what they called "bone head English". Most of the other classes that I took had to do with music.

One of my biggest dreams at that time was to major in music and piano so that I could someday play in "Carnegie Hall". Maybe too big a dream, but I had hopes, in my heart and soul I knew I could do it. Now that I was in college, I was once again in a special class. It had nothing to do with not pronouncing my S's, but now it was like learning a new language. It was learning to speak English correctly. All this broken English didn't help me one bit. It didn't matter as long as I could work towards my dream.

One of the classes I took was an introduction to music and piano. I really loved it and practiced on the piano whenever I could. I would go to the store and buy sheet music and piano books and just enjoyed playing the piano. One day my music professor called me in to talk to me, and he asked me why I was taking music classes, other than to learn more about music.

I thought it was an odd question, so I proceeded to tell him about my dream to one day play in "Carnegie Hall"; he looked at me and said "you will never attain that dream". Being from Hawaii and kind of shy to the ways of the world so to speak, I never bothered to ask him why he had said that to me. I just got up and said okay and walked out. My mind went back to grade school thinking of how kids had teased me because of my speech impediment, and I had that same feeling of failure because I couldn't talk well, and now here I was in my first semester of college and the professor was telling me I wouldn't reach the goal I was trying to reach. Maybe I would have reached it with some encouragement but that was such a letdown. God as my Guide knew what He was doing.

I thought that was some encouragement from a Christian college professor. Well that would be the beginning of the end for me at that college. I lost all interest in that school and eventually I dropped out. It was then that I decided there were other things to do in life then go to school and be miserable. Over forty years later I still wonder why he said that.

When I stepped out of the college scene, it was a time of love, a time of hate, a time of war, and there was no peace. Prior to coming to California, in 1966 when I was 17 years old, I had met a young Marine named Tony. He was stationed at the Kaneohe Marine Corps base and was waiting for his deployment to South East Asia; Vietnam. Everything about him I didn't like, but everything about him I loved. From the very beginning we were totally opposites.

To begin with, our religious affiliations were very different. Family wise he had a sister and a brother I had three older sisters and three older brothers. My Dad died when I was three, so I had one parent to raise me, my Mom. His parents were divorced when he was young, so he had two sets of parents. He was a city boy coming from the state of New York; I was from the little state of Hawaii. He was European; I was a Pacific Islander. He drank and smoked; I didn't do either.

As far as I was concerned he was cocky, sarcastic, and out spoken. I was the opposite. Now when I think about when I first met him, he wasn't cocky, sarcastic, or outspoken, he was just a confident person. When I first met him, he had already been on a helicopter, a plane and a train. Before I came to California, I could only imagine what it was like to be on a helicopter or fly in a plane or even ride a train. I mention these things so that whoever reads my book can see the difference to each of our backgrounds growing up.

Tony is originally from Albany, New York and was raised in Utica, New York. His life style was fast paced versus Hawaii, where my life style was slow and simple. You couldn't find two people that were so different in so many ways. I fell in love with the city boy and he in turn fell in love with the island girl.

Tony in Utica, New York.

For the thirteen months he was in Vietnam we wrote letters back and forth. He had wanted to marry me before he went to Vietnam, but I didn't want to become a Vietnam widow. Hawaii at that time was the R&R (Rest and Recuperation) for many that were returning back from Vietnam. Girlfriends, wives and family members would come to Hawaii to meet their family member that came back from Vietnam.

Three times I had received letters from Tony stating that he was going to come to Hawaii for R&R. The first time he said he was coming for R&R I was so excited that I was going to be seeing him. Not too long afterward I received that particular letter from him I got another letter from him telling me he wasn't going to be coming after all. The next time he was supposed to come I get another letter saying he wasn't making it because he got hurt. I thought he was never going to make it back to the United States.

Well by the third time he wrote and said he was coming to Hawaii for sure, I was apprehensive. When going to the airport to meet someone coming back from Vietnam it can be a very joyous or sad occasion as I soon would find out. Before his tour of duty in Vietnam would be up he would receive two Purple Hearts beside other commendations.

While waiting for Tony, there is a mixture of military guys and you just keep looking for who you are looking for until you find them. You can't tell who were going to Vietnam and who was coming back from Vietnam until something happened. So I was waiting like everyone else and there was so many guys going in all directions and then the sound like a gun went off. The reality of war set in; as I turned around half the guys hit the deck, civilians and other military personal just stood there. The guys that hit the deck were here either on R&R (rest and recuperation) or their tour of duty was over and they were returning home.

The reality of war is that when you are overseas sometimes you do not hear the words "incoming, incoming" you just automatically go down when you hear anything that sounds like a gun going off so that you don't get hit. When the guys from Vietnam realize that they were home, some of them got kind of embarrassed.

Looking around me I can't help but think, these guys are so young, their youth will be taken away from them, and they would have to live with whatever they saw and did in Vietnam the rest of their lives.

For those of us who have never been in war or in that situation, we cannot even begin to think what it is like, we can say we understand but we truly don't. We have never stepped on enemy ground. I have to thank those that are in the military for giving us the freedom that we might otherwise not have known. I would soon find out that War is no game, and what it would be like, being married to a combat Marine Corps Vietnam Veteran. The Vietnam War would play a role in our marriage and for the rest of our lives.

In May 1971, my first son Wayne was born. What could be more exciting to now have a child that we both wanted and loved? Tony didn't want me to work, and was making enough for us to live on. I wanted to stay home with my baby, so it was a done deal, the mother and homemaker. A couple of months after Wayne was born Tony wanted to move back to New York I didn't care where we lived as long as I had Tony and Wayne with me. By the summer of that year we packed and moved to Albany, New York. Going from Hawaii to California to New York was a jump for me. It would be another exciting experience in my life.

We had an old beat up brown station wagon, but to me it was my Cadillac and a ticket to an unknown place. We drove cross country and went through approximately 13 different states and our car broke down in practically every state. The first state after California that we drove to, as we pulled into a gas station, we were told to get to where we were going cause a tornado was on its way. I didn't know what it was like to be in a tornado, but the look and concern on my husbands' face meant we had to get out of there and fast.

We were young and in love with a baby and a whole new world before us. We drove cross country and kept my family in Hawaii abreast; especially my mom as to where we were in each state. Every state we passed through had its own flavor to it. With each state passing I couldn't understand why people wanted to go overseas when the United States had so many things to see, there are so many places to go to. You could travel the United States all your life and still not see all of it.

It would take us approximately five days to drive to New York, but five adventurous days it was. I was awestruck by everything that I saw. Finally we read a sign that said "Welcome to New York". This was not the New York I had expected. For me New York was all about big city lights and high buildings. Tony started to tell me different things about New York. He said we were going to upstate New York so don't expect big city lights where we are going.

Then I saw the sign Albany. Albany is not like the city of New York with high buildings and such. It was beautiful and Tony told me in a couple of weeks the Fall Season would be here; Fall Season, what was that all about? History wise, Albany is the oldest surviving European settlement from the original Thirteen Colonies and it is the capital of the state of New York.

After a couple of miles we pulled into the driveway of a three story house. I had never seen anything so beautiful and Tony said he was home. We were at his Dad and stepmoms house. This was not what I had expected; I guess

I was intimidated by the size and beauty of the house; there was the basement, the ground floor and an upstairs.

When we got out of the car he said, "Go knock on the door". I didn't want to get out of the car let alone knock on the door I was just intimidated by the size of the house. So I went to the door and after a couple knocks on the door, the door opened. This lady with red hair greets me and the first thing she said was, "Where's Tony?", then she gave me a hug and told me to come in, she said, Boots was not home yet; and then went to greet Tony. I can still see myself standing in the middle of this strange room with my baby Wayne, not wanting to move and let go of him in this strange house, and who was Boots? Then I could hear Tony talking to his stepmom; he was home in his environment and I knew now how he must have felt when he first met some of my family members.

Anyway, while I am standing there this Old Italian lady comes to me and starts talking Italian, and she said, "mangiare mangiare". I looked at Tony kind of dumbfounded, like "help" I don't speak or understand Italian. He said they had cooked and wanted us to eat. I whispered to him who is this little old lady and what is she saying. He said that was Grandma Galeo; his stepmother's mother and she wanted us to come in and eat. I told him I wasn't hungry and he said if you don't eat my stepmother will be insulted. When you go to an Italian house there is always food and to not eat or at least try something will not be in good taste.

Well, welcome to his world, and so the European and Asian Pacific world had now been brought together. I came to know and love Grandma Galeo, she would be the one person that I would spend I think the most while living at my in-laws and enjoyed her company so much. Half of the time I didn't understand what she was saying and when she looked and smiled at me, I wondered if she was thinking the same about me.

Within a couple of months the season changed from summer to fall and the leaves started to change colors. The colors were now changed from green to yellow, yellow to orange, and orange to red. It was something to behold.

Hawaii has its own beauty, tropical trees, waterfalls and all its colors and greenery, but New York has a beauty all its own with what I call the changing of the leaves. With the changing of the season came the changing of clothes. In Hawaii I was always in t-shirts, shorts, and barefoot. Now it was long pants and coats and warm clothing. This was going to be a challenge for me.

Fall didn't last very long before the winter season hit us. The winter we happened to be there was one of the worst winters New York had ever seen. Every day I turned on the television to watch the news they showed pictures on how high the snow was in different parts of New York. I couldn't believe my eyes, the snow had fallen and it was almost as high as the telephone phone poles. They showed two story homes that had icicles hanging at least 4 or 5 feet long. It is like it was caught falling off the roof and just froze.   I hadn't really seen snow fall except in California and then it was in the mountains, but to live in it never.

I felt like a kid in a new environment once again. Snow and icicles were just fun stuff for me I remember running under this icicle about 4 or 5 foot in length very excited yelling at Tony and Tony yelling at me to move from there. I mean I did not know the icicles could break off and kill me. We lived at my father in-law's house just for a couple of days, then found a house on Fleetwood drive to rent in the city of Albany, New York. The homes there were real nice although built differently from California, and really different from Hawaii.

After about a week we were finally settled in. It was the night before Thanksgiving and it started to snow and I thought "how beautiful." Although freezing cold when you stepped outside, the house was so warm inside. I went to sleep dreaming of everything that was happening in my life. The next morning I got up and opened the curtains and all I saw was white. Now when I was in California, I remember getting up and opening the drapes and everything was white. It scared me because I didn't know why it was so white. My sister told me the fog had rolled in.

When I looked out the window this time, here was a winter wonderland. It reminded me of a Christmas card. It was like the world had stood still for a moment and you could feel the crisp of the morning air, leaves frozen with ice, and icicles hanging never having time to reach the end of its journey but to be stopped in the cold, cold air, and see the beauty of God's creation. The street that we lived on had homes so different than from the ones I had lived in Hawaii and California. It reminded me of one of those magazine pictures that you see. There were some homes that were two stories high, screened in porch, beautiful trees lined the street and everyone had their lawns kept up nicely. The house we were renting wasn't two stories, but it had a basement which was something new for me.

Tony wasn't working that day because of a snow storm. I put some tongs with open toes on, and ran out the door and fell on the snow like a little kid. I was having so much fun and not paying attention to the neighbors. But as I looked at the neighbors' homes, one by one I could see them staring through the cracks of their curtain watching me but hoping I wouldn't see them. They probably thought I was crazy. It is the middle of winter and someone is in the snow with just tongs on their feet and wearing a house coat. Why? Doesn't everyone do that?

My husband was working three jobs at the time. During the day he would work as a construction worker. Rain, snow, whatever, after work he would come home and then went to his janitorial job in the evening. By the time he got home he just had enough time to shower, eat and then sleep only to be woken up by the alarm clock and start all over again. On the weekends he worked as a security guard; he was and always has been such a hard worker. He always wanted to be sure his family was provided for. I went from one loving person who took care of me, my Mom to another person that gave me the world, my husband.

Sometimes I would go with Tony to work, and would stay in the car with Wayne. I wasn't afraid of anything especially since Tony was the security guard. I remember this one particular night when I went with him. It was at a place where he felt we were safe enough that I could stay in the car with Wayne and it would be okay. Then it began to snow and snow. By the time Tony got to the car it had stopped. I was so excited telling him about the snow and I guess I just went on and on about how beautiful it made everything look.

Those are the times that hold such dear memories to my heart. A young couple with a baby, a husband working his heart out so that he could give me everything that I needed and wanted and more. Even after forty years of marriage he has never changed and gives me anything I want and more.

On the weekends when he wasn't working, we drove 90 miles to Utica, New York. Utica, New York was first settled by Europeans in 1773. The largest nationality group is Italians.

We spent time with my mother in law Vicky and her husband Frank. Although Frank was Tony's step dad, he considered him Dad. In Albany the Capital of New York, lived his real dad and step mom. Although life was wonderful and I had all that I could have asked for, I was now pregnant again. I wanted to move back to California where my sister Melinda and her husband Eddie, and my brother Wayne and his wife JoAnn and their families lived. So once again we packed up and moved back to Riverside, California. My stay in New York, although for only about a year gave me memories to last a lifetime.

October 1972, my younger son Frank was born. Both my boys were caesarean babies and I was told by the doctor that I would not be able to have any more children. My dream of having a little girl was crushed. But I had my two boys and the fact that they were healthy was more important than having a little girl.

I figured that one day they would grow up and one of them would eventually get married and would have a little girl. I have been blessed with two trophies my two granddaughters Nalani and Nelissa. They are Grandmas little girls and will always be her little girls; they are 13 years apart and I get to see life through their eyes.

My grand-daughters, Nalani on the left and Nelissa on the right.

My family became the center of my life. I had reached what most women want to obtain: a family, a husband who adored me, two boys, and good health. We were going to church and my husband had studied doctrines of the church, The Seventh Day Adventist. He continued to research the bible and how everything fell into place. He eventually was baptized into the church that I had been brought up with. God was my guide and my life was now complete.

Once again I became involved with the church. My boys were growing and doing more things with their friends which were fine with me. I became so involved with the church, I couldn't say no to anything that was asked of me, so I said yes to everything.

Soon my eyes went from God to the people of the church. Instead of going to church and enjoying the sermon and being blessed, the church became like a job to me. I was asked to help teach the kids class, sing special music, count the money, play the piano as church members were coming into the sanctuary, and it went on and on. I just didn't know how to say no; after all wasn't it for the Lord? I was always told that I was blessed with many talents.

If God had given me this talent, wasn't I supposed to use it, if it was to further His work? This was not what I had wanted. I wasn't even sitting in the church with Tony and the boys. Tony would ask me where I was going. It was always "someone needed help with something". I became the so called "minute man", and it was then that church became more of a burden then a joy. Tony never said anything, but I could tell he wanted me by his side during the church service. He didn't want to tell me I couldn't do what I was doing and I didn't want to tell the church members I couldn't help in anyway.

On the home front I realized my older son was getting into trouble almost every day in school. What was happening was he would be given assignments in class like the other kids but would be finish in no time. He would talk to the other kids which would get him and them into trouble. His teacher started to give him more assignments then the other students and he would still complete the assignments. He again would talk to his friends and get into more trouble.

So as parents, Tony and I were asked if he could take some testing to see what his scoring would be. After our approval and the testing, it was noted that his scores were extremely high for his age and that they wanted him to be put in the Gifted and Talented Education (GATE) program. So he was now put in the GATE program but continued to be in his regular class.

I would help my son do his homework, but now Wayne started complaining because he always had more homework then the other kids; I agreed with him. Talking to his teacher, I was told because he was in the GATE program he would have these extra assignments. To help the problem he was put in a higher grade. He kept up with the program but he was now with kids that were older than him. I began to get calls from his teachers and notices that he was being suspended left and right. We did not know what was going on, our family life had not changed and our other son had no problem as far as I could see.

Tony and I would talk about Wayne and the problems he was having in school. Tony had more of a feeling then I did as to what was happening and then he told me he thought Wayne was on drugs. I had never been around drugs so I didn't see it coming. I didn't want to hear what Tony had to say to me about Wayne and drugs; I just wanted to push it aside. Tony would try to tell me about drugs and what it can do, I guess deep inside I knew Tony was right, but for me it was heart breaking. Wayne had so much potential and being the kind of parents we were, we would have supported him in any type of education that he wanted. I keep pushing aside the thought that Wayne might be on drugs and talked myself into denying it.

Of course reality came knocking on my door and to my dismay we found out he was on drugs. His drug habits became more frequent until he became out of control. We took him to counselors and therapy. We had one on one therapy, group therapy, family therapy, individual therapy, etc. We tried to do whatever we could to help him kick the habit. We prayed constantly for him. He continued to do his drugs. I was ignoring my younger son Frank because he was doing well instead of spending more time with him and telling him how glad I was that he was not into drugs even though he was younger. I would argue with Tony constantly about Wayne. Wayne wasn't listening to anything we told him. He would stay out late and at times not even come home. I would worry and wonder how long this going to go on.

I remember going to our church to talk to our minister. The minister said we could put Wayne in the church school. We talked to the principal so that he knew what the situation was and he agreed that church school was what my son needed. My son's drug problem was discussed and we were told that was a personal thing and that no one would be told. He had talked to the other teachers about it and it was not going to be a problem as long as Wayne behaved in school.

We were told that there would be a weekly evaluation and we would take it a week at a time. I thought finally we were going in the right direction. I prayed that this would finally get our family life back to normal. The first week's evaluation the principal said Wayne was doing well in all his classes and the teachers were pleased with him and his participation in class. The other students liked him a lot and he just got along with everyone. I was just so happy Tony could go to work and not have to worry about me worrying about Wayne. I explained everything to Frank and he understood. My Frank always understood his brother.

Now when I see them together, I can't even imagine the things that had happened earlier in their lives.

Into the second week of school, I received a call from the principal and was told he needed to talk to Tony and me. As soon as we got to the school and sat down to talk to the principal my first question was how is Wayne doing in school? I was told that the teachers and students liked him and he was doing well in his studies; I knew that was not going to be a problem. So the next question was, why the telephone call? The principal sat there not knowing where to begin. He said one of the other student's mother found out about Wayne and his drug problem, and wanted my son out of the school. I wanted to know who it was, but they wouldn't tell me.

I asked the principal, how did anyone find out about the situation? It just happened that one of the girls in the school knew Wayne and his reputation. What I would hear next would change my thoughts on the Seventh Day Adventist church. The church that I had so loved the church that I had been brought up in. Through my 18 years in Hawaii, I had given so much of myself and had been so involved in all the activities of the church.

Now the Seventh Day Adventist church school, the church that I had been brought up to love, the church that had introduced me to a loving God, this church that was so much a part of my life, why? I was now told that because of this mother's complaint, Wayne would have to be removed from the church school and could not attend classes there anymore.

I didn't understand. I said to the principal "you're telling me he is doing well in all his studies as well as behaving in class, the teachers have no complaints, the students all like him, and this mother comes and tells you that she doesn't want him there anymore because he might influence the other kids to be bad!"   I was just floored.   I told the principal "but you are the head of the school."   The principal said he was sorry, and stated that Wayne could finish the week there and then that would be it.

Finish the week. Why finish the week? Now I had to tell my son that "hey, we put you in church school because of the problems you were having in public school, you're doing extremely well in your studies and your behavior, but they don't want you there because their afraid you're going to influence the whole school with your bad habits." How was I supposed to tell my teenage son this is the way it was. How was I supposed to tell him, yep that's what church school is all about, people and who they will influence. Was this mother running the school, and why didn't the principal support my son, or have a meeting with the church? Wasn't the church there to help young couples like us?

Tony knew by looking at me it was best not to say anything. I was floored; I was so angry, I walked out of the principal's office, walked off the church school lot and swore never to go to a Seventh Day-Adventist church again. Now I hated the church. I hated anything to do with the Seventh Day-Adventist, but most of all I hated God because I felt I had been let down, I had gone to His house, His home, I had gone to His people and I felt betrayed, Satan took over my life.

When I turned away from God and the Seventh Day Adventist church, unfortunately my sons turned away with me. My husband's faith grew stronger, and it never faltered. He continued to go to church and did a lot of praying. Our lives would now go in different directions.

My son's life would change after that. He got into more trouble and then he had to spend some time in Juvenile Hall. Juvenile Hall is an outpatient facility to help kids get back on track with their lives. What would have been just one stay in Juvenile Hall turned into many stays, heartaches for Tony and me and of course many crying sessions for me, and me questioning my life as a Seventh Day Adventist.

During that time frame I worked for the Department of Social Services. One day my boss called me in. We were not only co-workers but we had become good friends. She said "I want to show you something." To my surprise everything about my son and his records was recorded there on paper. She said I just wanted to let you know because your co-workers will be seeing this if they work on certain projects.

I thanked her and then I went to everyone in my section and told them about the problem that I had and to please if they had any questions to come and ask me and not to gossip about it. I worked for the Department of Social Services for about 6 years and during that time I think because of the talk I had with my co-workers, my son's problem did not become gossip and if they had any questions they would ask me. It made working there a lot easier for me and not to have to worry about anyone turning my son's case into something that it was not. In fact it turned out to be a blessing in disguise because I had other workers coming to me when they had problems with their kids.

I loved my job and my co-workers were the best. One day my boss told me there was a job opening at the Board of Supervisors for a typist clerk and told me if I wanted to I could take the test to see how I did. I said okay. A couple of days after the test I had a call and had been offered the job at the Clerk of the Board of Supervisors. The Clerk of the Board serves as the "clearing house" for the executive action of the governing authorities for the County of Riverside.

As much as I loved working at DPSS, I thought it was time to move on. I would be paid more and it wasn't too often that they had job openings at the Board of Supervisors. I had a big send off with so many of my coworkers attending my going away party. The Clerk of the Board position paid more and the job was a more prestigious job. Because of what we did and where we were located I got to see the public more. While working for the Board of Supervisors I was in charge of doing Legal Publication for the County of Riverside, as well as bid openings for the many County projects that were going on. There were a lot of other things that I did, but these were my main job duties.

Because of the legality of my duties I had the privilege of communicating with the different lawyers for the County. While working and taking care of my family I was going to college at nights and was thrilled when I received my Associate of Arts degree.

Because of what I was doing at work, and the people I was meeting, I became interested in the study of law. When I told Tony I wanted to go to law school and how he felt about it, he asked me if that is what I really want to do. I said yes and he said "go for it". My husband has always backed me up and had so much faith in me in whatever I wanted to do.

How was I supposed to go to law school and work at the same time? So I talked to some of the attorneys and they told me that there was a law school in Riverside, the only one that I could go to and still work since they had classes in the evenings. In fact some of the lawyers for Riverside County had attended the same law school. You needed a BA to get into the school but because of my job at the County and the knowledge I had, and the years at my job I was able to get in without a BA. I was thrilled, and wanted to get my Paralegal Certificate first. That way I would know if I really wanted to continue in the study of law.

Tony was heaven sent; he would support me in every way. He said "don't worry about anything just do what you have to do." My co-workers really supported me in any way they could. So began my journey in the study of law. Tony got off of work an hour before I did. He would then go home and check on our sons and tend to their needs and then do the cooking. When I got off of work, he would pick me up and would have my food all hot and ready on a plate and a cold drink. While he drove me to law school I would go ahead and eat my dinner.

Once he dropped me off at the school, he would go home and help me with the house work and do any laundry if there was any to do. Even though he was working himself he continued to support me in every way he could. After my classes were over in the evening he would pick me up and when I got home he always had everything cleaned up and ready for the next day. He would ask me what I wanted for breakfast so that he could have it ready for me. I would then take a shower, talk to my boys to see how things were going in their life and then hit the books. I would start studying about 11:00 pm at night.

On the weekends or whenever we found the time, he would drive me all over Southern California to go and buy any law books, tapes, videos, computer software or anything that I needed to help me in my studies. I got two or three hours of sleep at night. Luckily it didn't affect my job and how I performed. In fact even till today, if I get two or three hours of sleep that's enough for me.

Studying the law was so interesting and I tried to absorb everything that I learned either from my instructors or the other students. Finally the day came when I had to take my final exam when my grades were in and I had passed I was so happy and so was Tony. I didn't want to be a paralegal and work for someone else; I wanted to be a lawyer. By now my younger son Frank was out of high school and working.

Once again I had a decision on what my plans were for the future. Going to my husband, I told him I wanted to continue my study in law. It was something that we both had to think about, since he knew that he would have to be mother to the boys when I wasn't home and work and also help me with the housework. Again he told me is that what you really want? I said yes. Then he said "talk to the boys and see how they feel." Well they were involved with their own lives and whatever Mom wanted to do was okay with them.

That out of the way, Tony said he would support me but to pray and think about it, and when I made my decision he gave me his blessings. I quit work and continued on to get my law degree hoping one day to pass the Bar and become an attorney. Going to law school and studying law became my passion. I analyzed everything and anything that I read and it was either black or white and rarely gray. At times when my exams were coming up and I had to do more research and more study, I thought about my coworkers and how much fun I used to have at work and I missed them a lot. They had become my extended family and I kept in contact with them, and they always supported me in whatever I did.

When time permitted me, I would stop and visit for a while catching up with their lives, they were like family. Law school gave me a different outlook on life. It wasn't always what we could see or what we could hear but it was a lot about what we couldn't see or what we couldn't hear. I loved reading and during that period in my life I never read so much. Each word I read became a stepping stone to my dreams. The Black Laws Dictionary became my Bible and when I went home I would recite case after case to Tony, and like I adapted to his world as a Vietnam Vet, he adapted to my world of law.

Tony continued to help me at home by doing the cooking, laundry and anything else that needed to be done. When the world looked at me I had everything, especially good health. I may not have gotten any rest, but life was wonderful. My sons knew their Dad and Mom were always there for them if they needed anything. My world was now full of attorneys, and students that wanted to follow our instructors' footsteps.

It was at this phase of my life that I felt like an artist who turns the pages to start to paint a new picture. Now the colors were black, white and now even gray at times and so it was with the picture of my life. I wasn't sure what the future would hold for me, but I knew with my husband by my side, things would be okay and nothing could stop me to achieve my goal.

Now with an empty canvas, paint brushes and a pallet full of paint, a new picture would be painted. The artist dabs his brush into the pallet of paint, his eyes steady on the white canvas and concentrating on what he will paint, he begins to blend the colors together and then he takes his first stroke of the brush.

CHAPTER THREE
VIA DOLOROSA – Way of Suffering

"But rejoice to the extent that you partake of
Christ's sufferings, that when His glory is revealed,
you may also be glad with exceeding joy"
I Peter 4:13

In the American Heritage dictionary there are two words, "Via Dolorosa." It means a difficult course or experience. In Jerusalem it is known as the "way of suffering". This was Jesus' route from Pilate's judgment hall to Calvary.

For me, Via Dolorosa started around 1992. Everything had been going wonderful for me. My boys were old enough to do the things they wanted to do without our help, and my husband was busy with work. I had received my paralegal certificate and had continued on to law school. I was in my second year of the study of law. I was also giving private lessons in woman's self-defense. One of my dreams was to get a black belt in some kind of martial arts. Tony and I signed the boys' up to take lessons and we signed up in the adult class. There were two reasons for me to take martial arts. It would give me more time with the boys, and it was part of my Chinese heritage.

The martial arts that Tony and I were involved in were called "Kung Fu San Soo". Kung Fu San Soo, is not a sport and so we did not participate in any kind of tournaments or competition. I learned combinations of kicks, punches, strikes and leverages. When these combinations are directed to vital parts of the body, using balance, coordination and timing, they are extremely powerful and effective.

Using natural circular movements of San Soo, it made for a common sense fighting art. For females, it is the element of surprise for their attacker. While taking Kung Fu, I really paid attention to my weight and keeping it down. At this point in my life, nothing seemed threatening. I felt if I became a master in San Soo I would open up a self-defense school for woman. It would be strictly only for females. But I never got a master degree in San Soos and only got up to my Fifth Degree Black Belt.

The author practicing one of her high kicks.

Now that I was in law school I started having headaches, but it was only natural I thought. I had spent so many hours reading and studying for each class, each exam, and each discussion. I was trying to learn all the different laws and to keep up with the new laws. I thought between all the reading and studying and listening to these instructors a headache was part of the course. I grew up with the idea that I could achieve anything if I applied myself to whatever I was trying to achieve. A little headache was not going to stop me from continuing law school. To me it was always someone else who had it worse.

Sometimes I would tell Tony I had a headache, not telling him how bad it was. He would tell me to take a break, you're studying too hard. The headaches continued day after day, night after night. I was getting a little worried but that didn't stop me from doing what I had to do. If you asked me about a case or anything that was coming up in class, I could tell you the case forward and backward, inside and out. Since I like to debate, I would debate the subject if I disagreed with the other person. It was a challenge.

One specific night I went to class and I couldn't remember anything. I sat in the classroom dumb founded. One of my friends came in to borrow some notes and noticed something was wrong. Better see a doctor she said. I thought "what is a doctor going to tell me? I'm studying too hard, give me a break!" So like anyone who thinks there's nothing wrong with them, I put the idea of going to the doctor aside and struggled to do what I needed to do. I had always enjoyed law school.

As the days and weeks went by, I was struggling and having such a difficult time learning and I couldn't concentrate. Working on the computer (which at one time was so easy) was now getting more complicated for me. I just couldn't understand what was going on. I became frustrated because I couldn't even do the simple things. My headaches were getting worse and more intense as time went on. I started spending less and less time studying, and more time crying. I was trying to figure out what was wrong with me. Waiting for my husband in the car one day, I saw a former co-worker and waved to her. A sharp pain went through my head and it was awful. It was like someone had poked me with a needle and pulled it right through my eyes and head. I can't even remember if I told Tony, but by now he knew something was wrong. He was trying to convince me to go to the doctor.

I had two fears about doctors. First, I remember my father had gone to the hospital and I don't ever remember him returning home. He passed away and I thought why couldn't the doctors help him? I also had a fear of needles. In Hawaii in the 50's they used to give polio shots at school. I remember going for these shots, a student was screaming so much and started fighting with the nurse. Then the needle got pulled out of his arm. I will never forget that scene.

Tony told me "you really need to go to the Doctor." He knew what my fears were. I knew he would never tell me anything that was not good for me. Through my life and especially through my illness he has been so supportive of me. I never felt alone because he was always there. Later as my medical problems got worse he became my eyes, my ears, and soon had to talk for me. Because the pain was so bad and I couldn't study, I finally decided to drop out of law school. It wasn't an easy decision, but it was a decision that I had to do and decide on my own. All through our marriage, whenever I had an important decision to make, Tony always said, think about it, pray about it, then think about it again. He said, whatever decisions you make I will always support you. He never forced me to do anything I didn't want to do. He always guided me in the right direction, always giving me options.

The decision was made and I dropped out of law school. Another dream crushed. Because I didn't want to give up any of my law books, it would take another year before I got rid of most of my law books. All of the books especially the casebooks were still usable. I went to a law book store and got only ¼ cash of what I should have gotten. At this point I didn't care if I got nothing. My hope and dreams were shattered and life for me was so hard to understand. Instead of looking forward to the future of certainty I looked forward to a future of uncertainty. My husband was proud of what I had accomplished. In my eyes, and to me, the world would now look at me as a quitter, a failure, couldn't handle law school now you can't handle your life. I would now become the sick wife and I hated it.

I went to one doctor and would be sent to another doctor and then to another doctor, who would send me to a specialist. I went from one specialist to another specialist, from one medical facility to another medical facility, from one hospital to another hospital. I was given prescription after prescription. X-rays, MRI, cat scans, blood test, spinal taps, electrical shocks, light treatments, cortisone shots, it never ended. I hated doing the x-rays because I would be in pain and had to turn all over. I couldn't handle the MRIs because I was claustrophobic. Whenever I had to get an

MRI done I had to go to my neurologist to get injected to sedate me. Poor Tony had to rush me back before the sedation wore off so I could get my MRI done. If it wore off, I would be yelling and screaming and moving too much. The x-ray technician couldn't get a reading and so I would have to start all over again.

Taking blood from me was the worst. Of course I would have to take a lot of blood tests. I felt like anyone who took blood from me was a vampire just sucking the life out of me. I hated the needles and wanted to take and stab anyone who injected me. One of the nurses finally figured if they used a "butterfly" needle it might take a little longer but it would do the job because it was smaller and it would be just a little pinch. Every time I had new prescriptions there would be at least one in the group that I would have a bad reaction to it. Because I was going to so many doctors for different things, no one was keeping track of what doctor I was going to and what prescription I was given.

Nauseated all the time, I began to lose weight and started having a lot of skin problem. There must have been about 15 different creams, ointment, lotions and oils that I was given. Finally, I was sent to the chief dermatologist at the Medical Center I was going to. After seeing him I received a letter telling me that there was nothing he or any of his staff members could do to help me with the problems I was having with my skin.

My body was always in pain and agony. I couldn't sleep and would stay up all night and into the next day and developed insomnia. I was always so tired. My optometrist said my vision kept changing, and I was now told not to come back until I wasn't taking any more medications. I had gone to two optometrist and they couldn't figure the problems that I said I was having and being on so many medications didn't help. I was told they couldn't do anything for me. Another let down.

My face and head was always in pain. I was having more medical problems. I was told I had a pinched nerve in my neck and then there were problems with one of the discs in my back. In January of 1997, the doctor gave me a cane and a back brace hoping this would help me in some way. Fear set in with the cane because I kept thinking I was going to fall and sure enough I talked myself into tripping and falling. Putting on the back brace just wasn't going to do it for me. My nose would burn constantly; my right palm would just tingle every time I touched something. I always had electric like pains shooting to the left side of my face.

March of 1997, I woke up one morning and my nose started to bleed. I had never had any problems with bleeding noses. It stopped as fast as it started and I never knew when it would happen and so that became a problem. I was seeing so many doctors and didn't know who to tell. I started a chart so I could keep track of which doctor I was going to and for what reason and what type of medication they were giving me. How I did it in my state of mind and all the medications I was taking, it was a miracle I didn't overdose myself. God was still guiding me and I didn't know it.

Because of my back problem I was sent to the orthopedics. He put me on a tilt table and some dye was shot into my back. The results, I had arthritis in my back plus my disc in my back was leaking. The two alone was miner, but when there is a problem with both at the same time then it becomes a major problem. In between doctor visits I ended up in the emergency room so many times that I lost count.

My next doctor was an internist. By July of 1997, I was sent to another neurologist to get electrical shock treatment. I remember crying the entire session. A cat scan of my face and MRI of my brain was needed. I started going in for shots of 150mg of Demerol and 100mg of Vistaril at the same time. By now the fear of the needle had left me, but now I had another addiction; I wanted those medical shots and I knew that getting shots would give me some relief from the pain that was going through my body.

I became a starving animal that had not drunk for days and wanted those shots. I craved for shots and wanted more and more of the Demerol and Vistaril. They had found something that gave me some kind of relief. But like any medication you can only take so much before the Doctor tells you, "No more! Enough is enough!"

Because of seeing so many doctors, I was being given so many different medications. I kept track of them so that I wouldn't over dose and made sure as soon as I took it I would cross it out. I became a prescription drug addict, and it was being given to me legally. I hated it because my oldest son Wayne had become a street drug addict. Now I felt that it was the Devil's way of mocking me telling me "You should have listened to me then you wouldn't be in the position you are in."

My Primary Care Doctor referred me to a Neurosurgeon to get his opinion. After taking some test the results came back. I had "Trigeminal Neuralgia". Trigeminal Neuralgia is when a blood vessel touches the trigeminal nerve where the nerve enters the brain. The pain is worse than a migraine and could be triggered by anything. I was told I needed brain surgery.

Being alive for me was agonizing. When I blinked my eyes, it was as if someone was poking my eye with an ice pick and never letting it shut. My mouth felt like the dentist had ripped all my teeth out and had given me nothing for pain. My nose would burn so badly, it was as if someone was pouring hot sauce into it. When I cried, it just made everything worse. The pain was now happening all the time and all at once and anything and everything triggered it.

Taking Oramorph and Percodin, my prescriptions were written in triplicates. I had to be registered as a drug addict, but a legal one. I continued to get shots of Demerol and Vistaril. With all the medication that I was taking, the pain would still be there. My brain surgery was scheduled for November 3, 1997. I had to go to the blood bank to give blood. I had told the workers there that I hated needles and they would have a hard time getting the blood out of me. Of course they didn't believe me. The workers there had such a hard time trying to get blood from me and I think some of them were starting to get real frustrated.

I have floating veins. Floating veins can be very deceptive, a spot can be located where the entry looks good but as soon as the needle is inserted the vein moves. On my right hand they tried to get some blood out and some blood was taken out. I think that day they needed 5 little tubes. They tried endlessly to get more blood from my right hand, but they were getting absolutely nothing. I think so much had been taken out there, there was no more to give. They then tried to take blood from my left hand; but that still didn't work.

The workers kept poking and poking me all over to get the blood started. The first person couldn't do it so they called another helper, and then another helper, but they still couldn't get enough blood to fill the tubes. For all the pain I went through, I was then told the blood could not be used because there was not enough and all it did was leave me crying and in more pain. My only option was to find someone to donate blood. I had a lot of donors but no one I knew at the time had the same blood type as me. The individuals that did have the same blood type as me, for one reason or another couldn't give.

I went in for pre-opt, and during pre-opt two spots were found on my lung and one spot was found on my right side wall chest. The brain surgery was cancelled and the suffering became worse. Now I seemed to always be strung out on prescription drugs. I was sent to another doctor an Internist among others to see how and what could be done to ease my pain. During this time more blood work, MRI, CAT scan, etc. were done on me. My whole life was like living in a fog and not being able to find my way out.

On the 15 of December 1997, I had to go in for a needle biopsy on my chest. To put me out I was given Valium pills, shots of codeine, morphine through the IV and some other type of medication. I called this the inch by inch biopsy. They had me lie on my stomach then injected me with medication, put me through the MRI machine, than a picture, then pulled me out and injected me again. This is how the procedure went and since I had never had it done that way, my mind was totally confused.

Because everything was timed, I had to be sedated and put out and the procedure had to be done before the medication wore off. On one occasion none of the individuals that were in the room checked to see if I was completely out. The medication was enough to make me groggy but I was still awake, but couldn't talk. I couldn't tell them I could feel the needle when I was injected. I could feel the morphine going through my veins, and I could hear the doctor talking to the person that was helping him. I wanted so badly to tell them, "Listen to me, I'm still awake! I'm still awake can't anyone hear me?" I was too numb with drugs to move or speak and so I suffered alone.

My brain surgery was put on hold, and I was now strictly on morphine and getting more shots of who knows what. If I ended up in Urgent Care Clinic or the emergency room they would only give me shots of Vistaril with Stadol. It would give me comfort for a little while but then the pain would start up again. I went to bed with pain, I got up with pain, and I had pain even when I was sleeping.

I got up around 4 am one morning. My eyes were so watery, my nose was stuffed, and my throat was burning so bad I couldn't swallow. The left side of my face started to burn like crazy, and my right hand was throbbing. I just wanted them to do the brain surgery and get things over with. Maybe all the pain would go away and I would get some relief.

I would be so hungry and would eat too much and then I would get sick and throw everything up. There was no limitation for or against anything. My weight was fluctuating up and down. I didn't even care what I looked like. I hated looking into the mirror because what I saw looking back at me was horrible. I stopped calling family and friends and soon would become more of a hermit except to my sons and their families. There were more blood tests to come and I thought "how much more blood can they get out of me?" In my head anyone who took blood from me was a vampire just draining and draining blood from me, sucking the life out of me and I could not fight back.

I had lost so much weight, I felt and looked awful. Tony would take my picture whenever he could and in his eyes I was still his beautiful wife. I would try to smile for him but I was in so much pain all the time.

On the 31st of December 1997 I had an appointment with one of the many doctors that I was constantly seeing. I was told he was going to do a biopsy under my right arm, because of what was shown on the x-ray. I was suffering with so much pain. I had come a long way from when I took my first injection, but the needle the doctor used for the biopsy had to be one of the largest that I had ever seen. I had to be injected several times and with each injection the screaming that came out of me would have sent chills down anyone's back. Tony came in to see why I was screaming and even he thought the needle was the biggest he had ever seen. All he told me was that I had to be injected no matter and, there was no choice. No choice! No option! That was my life.

After I got home I remembered lying in bed wondering "Why?" With all the injections and medications I was taking for pain, which were to give me comfort, nothing was working. Even the morphine that I was given just did nothing for me. Before the end of the day with the medications not working I would be back in my neurologist's office for more shots of Demerol and Vistiril to help with the pain. I would leave the office just as zoned out as can be thinking "No wonder people keep taking drugs: It kills the pain for just a little while, then you get hooked on it and need more and more and will do anything to get it if you are physically and mentally able to do so."

It seemed like all my medication was now counteracting each other. I didn't have sense enough to tell all these doctors what pills I was taking and that I had so many. I just assumed all the doctors knew which pills had been prescribed to me. Couldn't they see the way I was, the way I looked?

By January of 1998, I was so disconnected with everything. My face was so sensitive any little thing would trigger agonizing pain; even the soft breeze. I started to get a hoarse voice producing sounds that could not be understood. My throat would sting when I took anything; it didn't matter whether it was medication, drinks, food, or swallowing my own spit. The morphine was making me dizzy and sick to my stomach all the time. My skin was drying up. Then it would crack and start bleeding. There were many times when the cuts and cracks would be so bad they were like open wounds and nothing could be put on it to help ease the pain. I would just cry and cry and all I could see through my tears was bloody open skin. I felt worse because my husband wanted to help me so badly but there was nothing he could do.

He would spend hours holding me like a little baby and rocking me to sleep. He would be so tired from staying up night after night, and worrying if he was going to lose his wife. On days when I felt good enough to stay home by myself and he felt comfortable with it he would go to work. He was always calling me to see how I was doing. If I didn't answer the phone he would come home only to find me sleeping. Tony would take time off to take me from one appointment to another. Then there were the many times that he would be rushing me to the doctor's office, medical clinic or to the emergency room. It seemed like there was no time frame; days would run into weeks and weeks into months.

At this time my brain surgery was still on hold. Now different individuals were telling me I needed to get anointed. Well to me, the only time a person was to get anointed was when they were about to die. Being that I was on morphine and as ill as I was, that was the first thing that would come to my mind. Was I going to die and no one was telling me? I quickly put that thought aside.

My mind was always playing tricks on me; I would hear voices and see things that no one else saw but me. I remember Tony said, "I'm going to take you for a ride maybe you'll feel better." We were on the 91 freeway going anywhere from 70 to 80 miles an hour. To me, normally that would have been just the speed he should be doing. All of a sudden I started to hallucinate and thought someone was talking to me. I turned to my right side and I swear there was a person telling me to open the door so that they could talk to me. I started talking to this imaginary person and then I tried to open the car door. It never dawned on me that the door was locked and no matter how hard I tried the door would not open. Tony realizing what was happening, started to yell at me.

Now in my mind I had two people on both sides of me yelling. One person was saying open the door, the other person was saying don't open the door. What was I doing wrong? Then I turned to look at my left side and could see Tony saying, get away from the door. Coming back to reality, I just sat in the car and stared out the window. That would be the end of going for rides.

Whenever I thought about God, I wondered, why should God want to either heal or help me since I had turned away from Him? Finally, I called a friend who's like a mom to me and her husband is like a dad to me. Fred (who has since passed away) and Jane have always been like my guardian angels. Years ago Jane and I had worked together. I would call Jane up crying and telling her about the pain I was going through. "Why Jane," I would cry, "why?" What have I done so wrong in my life that I have to go through this awful situation? Jane would spend hours talking to me and telling me everything was going to be okay and she would just listen as I rambled on and on, just listening to me. I was like a tape recorder that would never stop.

I don't know how the word anointment came up in our conversation but she said to come to her house and she would call her pastor from Arlington Seventh Day Adventist Church. I thought okay, I really trusted her and felt that whatever she was telling me was okay.

On January 10, 1998 it was decided that I would be anointed. The devil must have been horrified to think I was actually or other people were actually asking God to heal me somehow. This would be one of the strongest battles that I would have to fight with the devil. It was 2:50 am on the 10th of January when I woke up and saw absolutely nothing. Somehow the devil was able to sneak into my weak and shattered mine causing me to think I was going blind.

I started running around in circles screaming, "I can't see, I can't see, oh please God don't let me die this way, not in pain, not blind." Tony didn't know what was going on at first and didn't know what to do. He watched helplessly as his wife ran in circles and continued to do so like a mad person.

Running around I stopped in the middle of the room and found a piece of paper and with a marker started to write my name, why, I don't know. As I wrote there was nothing or at least in my mind nothing was showing up on the paper. Tony kept yelling and telling me; "You wrote your name honey", I can see it, and it is there, look." I kept looking and looking I still couldn't see any writing and I became more hysterical as I kept banging into things like a blind person who cannot see anything in front of them. I could hear him calling my neurologist in a panicked voice and telling him what was happening. The doctor had told him to get me to the emergency right away and he would call them ahead of time.

By now I was screaming I was going to die. The devil was after me because I was getting anointed; why did I ever decide to get anointed? Till today I don't know how Tony got me into the car. All I can remember was sitting in the car. I was fearful of everything and would hide my face in my hands. Every time I opened my eyes the trees looked like wooden people trying to cover the car up. Tony must have gone through several red lights. I don't remember when I got to the hospital or whatever happen but after several hours things calmed down. Once again I was in the emergency room. Later we found out that I had a withdrawal from a medication I had been taking. But I still believed it was the devil, Satan himself.

I thought after the incident could I ever get off of any of the medications that I was taking without horrible incidents happening to me. I thought I would live and die taking medications for the rest of my life. It was like living in a nightmare that just wouldn't let up.

I decided not to do the anointment. I felt awful. I looked like death and inside I was a mess and I was so fearful of the devil. I thought the devil had finally gotten a hold of me. I was scared and frighten. I called Jane up and told her what was going on. Somehow she convinced me to come to her house. God would protect me. Tony and I ended up at her house and there I was introduced to the Pastor of their church and his wife. I don't remember much of anything, what I said or did. I was still kind of doped up from the shots that had been given to me. I was in tears because every inch of my body hurt. In other words, I was a complete mess as a human being.

I looked around and saw some familiar faces. There were others I didn't recognize. Somehow in my mind I knew they were supportive and you could see a lot of love and yet you could see a lot of sadness in their faces. Whatever happened during that time I don't remember and the only ones that know are the people that were there and till today they have never spoken of it. With the anointment out of the way, I was still in so much pain.

After I got home I just laid in bed and started wondering how long it would be before my husband would leave me. I wouldn't blame him one bit. In fact it would have made things a lot easier if he didn't love and care for me as much as he did. He went through Vietnam and had seen enough pain and suffering and now to come back home, get married and be stuck with a wife that was ill and have to be mother and father to both our sons. Was there truly a God of love out there?

Where was this Seventh Day Adventist God? Had I grown up to worship a God that never really existed except in my mind? Yes I had gone to church. I had grown up in the church. Was this all a figment of my imagination? Was the Devil actually my God? Confusion started to settle in as I laid there in bed.

As the days went by and my life was like a big twister, something was now happening to my skin. My face would just start bleeding and my arms did the same; blood would just appear out of nowhere. I knew I hadn't scratched myself or anything, but I would bleed. Sometimes I would look in the mirror and it looked like someone had poked needles in my face and I would just start bleeding. I was worried that another medical problem had started and why was this was happening.

My face would get so red at times it looked like I had put rouge on it. So I was back in the doctor's office with this new health problem. After doing some testing, what was happening was that my capillaries; the minute blood vessels that connects the end of the smallest arteries with the beginning of the smallest veins, was bursting inside of me. It was causing me to bleed through my pores. It would freak me out when it occurred. Even though it didn't happen daily, it happened enough times to scare me. I was afraid to go anywhere and have people not only see me the way I was but then to start bleeding in front of them. To have to constantly repeat things to people and tell them why and what was happening to me became tiresome to me.

There were so many times when I was in a fog. I couldn't tell day from night, morning from evening. The pain in my face was so bad I just wanted my eyes close and even then there was pain. Tony now had to become my eyes, making sure I had the right medications and I ate the right things. I was so drugged up with prescription drugs or injections that I couldn't comprehend a lot of things that were said and were happening to me. I didn't care about anything except wanting more of anything to take the pain away. The drugs and injections were now my life savers as far as I was concerned.

My husband was there for every appointment, surgery, emergency and daily chores. He had to answer telephone calls at home. When we were with other people and I did talk I would ramble on and one or say things that no one could understand. Tony had to now become my voice to the medical people, family and friends that were constantly asking questions. I don't know how he functioned at work.

In fact, had Tony not have helped me in remembering things, I would never have written this book. What I say and did was one thing. What he saw as the months and years went by was another thing. He would be talking to me but I couldn't hear him. It was as if his mouth was moving but no sound was coming out, I could understand bits and pieces. I do remember him telling me as much as I could to keep track of whatever was happening and the medications I was taking. This way, I guess he could see what I was doing while he was at work or if any of the Doctors needed information then I would have something to show them.

My grand-daughter Nalani, she was the only thing that brought
sunshine into my life at the time, and would be so sad when I wasn't
feeling good. She would say, "Grandma I will take care of you",
and she was only four years old.

I would scribble things down no matter where I was, no
matter what I was doing, day or night. I did the best as I
could, but there were times when I would scribble things
down and then be frustrated because I couldn't read my
own writing and then would spend so much time dissecting
each sentence so that I could understand and know what
was happening in my life.

I kept track of the doctors I saw also. There are many
things that also happened to me that I left out. God allowed
me not to remember everything but just enough so I could
write this book and tell my story. I could have gone and
got my medical files but it would have been too expensive
to have it copied. When I got a prescription, I would jot
down what it was, why I was taking it, what doctor, and
so forth.

Every time I thought things were going to be okay, something else would come up. I continued bleeding from my pores; and so it was back to the medical clinic for chest x-ray, blood test, EKG, urine samples, etc. I was now scheduled on the 22nd of January 1998 for surgery. At the time I couldn't quite understand why I was having surgery performed on me, except that it had to be done. All I knew was it had to do with the biopsy that had been taken from under my right arm. The doctor did an "excisional right chest wall mass surgery."

After I came out of the surgery and was in my hospital room I was told by my doctor that a tumor that was bigger than the size of a soft ball was taken out of the right side wall chest; it was called a "schwannoma". Schwannomas are benign nerve sheath tumors. When these tumors begin to grow, they displace and compress adjacent nerve fascicles within the nerve. Mostly they are solitary and occur sporadically. Now I knew why I had such pain and numbness in that area. Tony and I were shocked to say the least. I was in the hospital for about a week. I found out it wasn't cancerous but could have developed into cancer if it had not been removed. Till today I can't figure how it grew inside of me and I didn't even know I had it. I was given more morphine for the constant pain that I had. When I got out of the hospital it was back to a normal routine of getting shots of Demoral and Vistaril but still continuingg to have pain.

My brain surgery was rescheduled. I had to start all over again with pre-ops, taking blood test, running down to the blood bank, etc. I was still trying to recuperate from my arm surgery, but the brain surgery was needed badly so I went ahead with it as soon as I could. This was about six weeks after the doctors had removed the tumor in my chest wall. The surgery went like clockwork. I didn't want anyone coming to the hospital to see me. I was embarrassed by the way I looked and felt just awful. I knew they were going to shave off most of my hair and that was hard to swallow. It was like a part of me was getting cut off. The last two faces I saw were my husband and my adopted mom Jane. My husband and always left me with a smile, but I knew deep inside their hearts must have been aching for me but there was nothing I could say or do.

Before I went in for my brain surgery, I had requested that since my hair was long enough to make a wig that when it was cut would one of the nurses please put the cut hair in a bag. I would then give it to the cancer society. There is a place where wigs are made from human hair for people who have lost their hair because of cancer. I felt that at least it would be put to good use. When the surgery was over and I was coherent the first thing I asked was for my bag of hair. Evidently one of the nurses thought it was thrash and threw it away. When I was alone I just cried and cried; another dream to help someone was crushed because of someone else's carelessness.

When I lay in bed my head was so numb. It scared me because I couldn't feel anything on the left side of my head, but I could feel on the right side of my head. I felt so unbalanced, like a teeter totter. I was afraid to move my head. When I looked up or sideways with my eyes all I could see were white bandages.

I was to stay in the hospital for at least a week to nine days or more; it all depended on how things were going. I don't usually like to put things or situations in a bad light, but the experience I had at the hospital intensive care unit would be my worst nightmare; maybe this one night was just a bad night for everybody.

The evening of my surgery, my younger son Frank came and stayed with me. Every time I turned he would be sitting there reading a magazine. If I needed anything I would just ask him. I started to feel a lot of pain and asked the nurse who was in the room to give me more medication. She said she would check my chart and come back. I told my son he could leave. Frank said "Are you sure Mom? I can stay." He had to go to work the next day and it was getting towards midnight. He said, "Mom, are you sure you want me to leave? I could stay till after they give you your medicine?" I wanted him to stay, but I just didn't want my son to see me in so much pain and I didn't want him to miss work. Till today I regret that I ever told him to leave, maybe what happened next would not have happened.

After my son left it was about a half hour before the nurse came back in. She proceeded to tell me what she was going to do. She told me about putting the medication through an IV and explained different procedures to me. As I laid there and watched her she was having a hard time getting the IV started. The nurse could not find a vein to poke the needle in and she kept poking me all over. She was just having a hard time and I couldn't understand why.

After a while I told her to get another nurse. The second nurse came in and she was having problems trying to start the IV also. Now the first nurse told me she would go and get another nurse. The third nurse came in and like the other two was having problems. Every time one of the nurses thought they had the IV started the veins would collapse. They should have known I had floating veins.

Floating veins are very deceptive. At the point of entry with the needle it will move and then you have to try to find another vein to start all over. It was bad enough that I was hurting. The poking of the needle felt like stabbing pains every time they tried to start the IV. By now, with three nurses trying their best to start this IV, I was in tears and screaming. I thought if they could not get the IV started, and I kept screaming, staples they used for my brain surgery would come out. I was just scared.

Finally, I had enough. My hand was now hurting worse than before I had come in. I told them to get out, to leave me alone. I couldn't understand why they hadn't called my doctor or even my husband to tell them what was happening. Well I got my wish. They left me alone. All three of the nurses left.

Now I had a problem. I couldn't move and any movement would cause me so much pain. I would now lie in bed agonizing and crying. At that point I couldn't even scream. I wanted to call my husband but the phone seemed miles away. How would I ever get to call my husband or any of my doctors? I didn't care which one. I needed help. So I decided to turn and lean on the rails and somehow maneuver my way to the phone. In their rush to get out, the nurses had forgotten to put the rails up and when I turned, I almost fell off of the bed. Now in the dark of the night, I knew the nurses would not be back and probably thought I was one of their worst patients.

One of the many, many times I ended up in the hospital. I would gain weight, than the next time I would lose so much weight. Tony would always be there for me. He hated to leave and of course after he left, the tears would just flow. It had always been the two of us and now we were separated due to circumstances beyond our control.

I looked at the clock on the wall and for about six hours I suffered more then I or anyone in my condition should have had to. I just laid there wishing that it was my time to go; just get it over with. Finally a nurse came in. They had changed shifts and through my tears I told her what had happened. She went out of the room so fast and I thought "Oh great now this nurse is gone." Thank God she came back real quick and gave me something to help ease the pain. When Tony called and I told him what had happened, he was at the hospital in no time and very angry. I told him another nurse had come in the morning and gave me something for the pain which was helping and by the way, how did he get in? It was not visiting hours yet. Knowing my husband, it would be very hard to keep him away from me especially since he now knew what had happened.

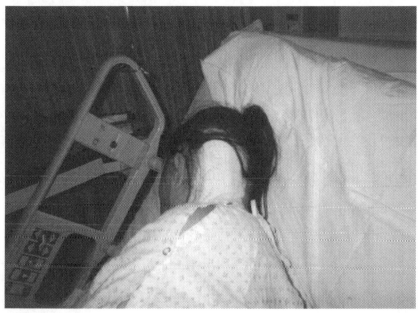

As you can see the way they had me bandage up, the left side of my head felt like I had a brick block on my head. It was horrible.

Finally at peace with myself and finding some comfort I told Tony to go to work. I would probably sleep all day and he was only a phone call away. He was about six blocks away from the hospital if I needed him. Seeing to it that I was comfortable and of course instructing the nurse on certain issues he went to work and I fell asleep.

About 10 in the morning during his break he came to see how I was doing and asked me if I had eaten. I said no.

He said, why not? I said they left the food tray, but with my right hand still hurting from the other operation, my left hand with all kinds of IVs in it, and my head numb, I couldn't feed myself so they took the tray away. I could see the anger in his face already and he called the nurse to come into the room. When she did, he asked her why she took the food away. She said "your wife was sleeping, so I took it away." After a 15 minute lecture from my husband about the dos and don'ts as far as his wife was concerned, he said he would be there to feed me morning, noon and in the evening. They were not to take the food tray out no matter what the circumstance was or they would have to deal with him.

Well, I should have known what would happen, because the service only became worse. By the third day, I wanted out of the hospital. My husband said there was no way they were going to let me out so soon. I felt awful. When I had visitors I couldn't remember who came and who didn't. There is nothing worse than lying in bed sick, helpless and people come to visit and you just look awful. I was not talking coherent. I didn't know who was who at times I didn't know who I was; I mean the medication just took over.

Having this big old bandage covering most of my head, I must have looked a sight. I told Tony and the nurses I didn't want to see anyone except my granddaughter Nalani every day. At that point in time she was the only light of my life and I needed her. At such a young age, she was being Grandmas, Special Angel, a name her Grandpa has given her ever since. She was special and as little as she was she would come to the room when they let her and would jump in bed with me. She was never frighten of the way I looked.

When everyone left I would call Tony. After I hung the phone up I would either cry myself to sleep or just cry period because my head was numb and it was scaring me. The left side of my body was in pain, the right side of my body was in pain and I felt so all alone. I couldn't do anything; it was such a helpless feeling. Where was God? I need you God, have you turned away from me? Where are you?

Going to the bathroom was the pits. I had to have a nurse with me whenever I went (which I hated), because of the type of surgery I had. I had this IV hooked up that I had to drag along with me which is normal, but because of my brain surgery I felt like I had a cement brick on my neck and it was going to fall off at any time. One side of my head was normal but the other side was just numb but hurting. It was such a very weird feeling. I just couldn't balance the way I walked. It was like walking and feeling like you is going to fall sideways but you don't.

At nights when I was lying in bed and the street lights or moon light would shine through, I thought, "why me Lord?" During the day when visitors were gone, I would look at all the beautiful bouquets and cards that were set up and thought how kind people were to me.

When I came home Tony brought all the cards and letters home.
There were also so many bouquets that we left some at the hospital
for other patients who had nothing. I was so blessed and yet I
couldn't see the light at the end of the tunnel.

When my doctor came in to check on me, I was told,
"before you could go home Mrs. D'Aprile, we need to know
that you are able to walk well, besides some other things," so
a couple physical therapists would come in and work with
me and help me to walk again. The doctor said it would
take a while for me to feel kind of normal again. When
they left, I thought a while. "No he's crazy." So I decided
when no one was around I would get up and try to walk
by myself.

The first day I tried to walk I almost fell flat on my face, IV and all. I was so unbalanced like a bowling pin rocking back and forth. As soon as I was alone and was sure the nurse was not going to come in I began to slowly walk around the room, holding on to anything I could. Every agonizing step, inch by inch, tears would run down my face angry at the world to be in the situation I was in. I was angry at God because He was my healer but where was he? This was not my God! I was angry at Satan for not taking my life.

I did not like the service at the hospital, especially for an ICU. The nurses were nice but some of their methods just had to go. Unhappy with the way I was being treated, by the third day, I had had it. They were always late in bringing my pain medication and by the time they brought it the pain was worse and so the medication that they gave me didn't work. The anger that was building up inside of me was not good, because it was just stressing me out. I called my husband and told him I wanted out. He said, "But you just had surgery on Tuesday and it's only Friday morning." I didn't care. I wanted out and knew that he could take better care of me then how I was being treated and cared for.

That night he came to visit and once again I pleaded with him and told him that I wanted out of this hospital. He said okay. He would talk to my doctors and see what they said, but I also knew he would do anything in his power to get me out of there. Saturday morning he was up at the hospital bright and early. When he walked into the room, he had this shocked look on his face but it went from a look of shock to a look of anger. I was smiling even though hurting and couldn't understand the look on his face or why he was so angry. My husband could not believe what he saw.

When they did the surgery, they had to put 25 staples on my head to hold together where they had had to cut open my head. Someone, and of course no one would take the blame, had taken the bandage that was covering my staples off and had gotten a paper towel and had put it on. Holding the paper towel down, they had taken regular scotch tape and tried to tape the paper towel all over my head. Because my head was so numb and I was so dopey all the time I didn't know what anyone was doing to me.

It was the most unsanitary thing that could have happened to me or anyone else after a surgery. But for a brain surgery, you have to have been stupid or ignorant to let something like that happen. Later I had people tell me I should have sued the hospital because where they had cut me open could have become infected and so on. I have never believed in suing anyone. I always felt there is a reason why things happen or do not happen to anyone.

Anyway as the saying goes, the ball started rolling. They knew by the look on Tony's face and the sound of his voice he was angry and he went to the nurses' station and told them to call my surgeon and my neurologist. They kept telling him it was Saturday, and they could not get a hold of the doctors. He didn't care. He wanted both doctors there pronto. It was like everybody was going to lose their job if the doctors were not there. Well within half an hour both my doctors were at the hospital.

I knew the doctors were not too happy, but they also knew Tony. He was adamant, unyielding in his attitude because I had wanted out, and because of the way I had been treated. He was going to get me out of there. The surgeon was against me going home so soon. He didn't want to be responsible for anything that happened at home. I did not want a nurse to come home with me or come once a day, and if anything happened how fast could we get to the hospital? We only lived about 10 minutes away from the hospital but anything could happen. The doctor was so hesitant, his reputation was on the line should anything happen. My neurologist, bless him, said that Tony could take better care of me than anyone could.

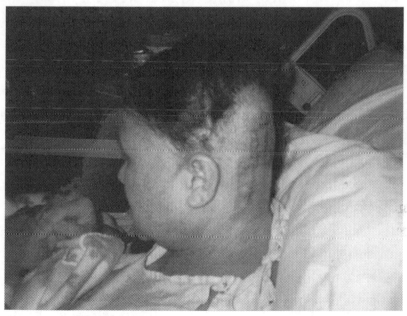

Tony had a picture taken before they bandaged it up again.

My surgeon finally agreed to let me go on the condition that I could walk among other things. All the practicing I did at nights when no one was around had worked out for the best. Of course I was not walking straight; it was hard because of the things I was hooked up to, and my head being so numb I couldn't feel anything. My surgeon was surprised given the situation. Once again my neurologist said that Tony could take better care of me at home. His office was just about 3-5 minutes from my house and he could be contacted right away. Finally it was agreed that I could go home, I was so happy but in so much pain. At least if I was going to die then let me die at home.

Once I got home there were big decisions to make. Tony said he would take the time off to be with me. I didn't want him home with me. 24/7 would not have worked as far as I was concerned. So he said I'll send for one of your family members from Hawaii to come and stay with us, but I fought him on that issue all the way. There was no way I was going to have anyone see me in the condition I was in. I looked terrible. I was strictly on morphine among other things and it was putting me in terrible mood swings. No one would have wanted to be around me after 5 minutes.

My husband was doing everything humanly possible to give me comfort. He would call me from work, come home on his breaks and lunch to see if everything was okay. He would fix me snacks before he went to work so I had things to munch on. I knew from the look on his face that he hated walking out the door every morning to go to work. I told him I would sleep all day. Of course, I wanted him to be with me but I felt he needed a break from me.

The realization of actually being sick and needing help came when Tony left for work one day. I remember getting up to go to the bathroom. I got real dizzy and tripped and went flying into the wall. So that I wouldn't hit my head, I went down on my left hand because my right hand was still hurting from the earlier surgery that I had. When I finally came to a stop, I thought I had broken my wrist. My left knee was hurting. I had skinned it real good and had a big old shiner. Needless to say when Tony got home and I told him what had happened he was so upset. Not with me, but with the fact that he wasn't there and thinking that something worse could have happened.

The only person I wanted to see at the time was my only grand-daughter Nalani. She always brightened my day. She even told me it was okay that they cut my hair, and I could have some of hers. When Frank brought Nalani, she would just sit next to me and play with her dolls or color. She never complained. When I went to sleep, before I dosed off she would say, "Did you take your medicine grandma?" Before she took a nap with me she would check to see if I wanted a blanket or if my pillow was okay, and would arrange her Barbie dolls so that they could sleep with her. She was my "Special Angel." God had brought a 4 year old to show me the way and more, that even a child could lead me. Her kindness and love brought us so close till today and she is just as sweet and kind as she was then.

The 30th of March was the day my stitches were to be taken out. It just happened I also had an appointment to take a nerve test since my right hand was always in pain; pain was a part of my life 24/7. My appointment was to be in the late afternoon. Well, if I didn't have bad luck I would not have any luck at all. I was lying on my pillow and wanted to get up for something. As I started to get up I felt like someone had pulled my head back. I couldn't figure out what was wrong. I tried to get my head up off the pillow and again I couldn't. Because my head was still numb I kind of panic. As I ran my hand over my head I realize that one of the staples had come lose and was stuck on the pillow case.

The phone was on my right side but I couldn't turn my head. My left hand was still sore from the needles that I had been poked with. I couldn't move my right hand because of the pain that had continued to bother me from the prior surgery. At the end of my foot there was a pair of scissors which my husband had left when he had to change the dressing on my head.

Somehow, and till today I don't know how, I managed to do what I did. Crazy as it sounds, I maneuvered my left big toe in to the hole of the scissors handle crying with each move because of all the pain and bent my leg so I could get the scissor with my left hand. I figured if I put my right hand under the pillow close to my head, pushing my hand into the pillow it would hold the other staples in, so would not be pulled out and come off of my head. Of course what I did next was really stupid. Not seeing where I was cutting, I started to cut the pillow case around the staples. I can't believe that I didn't end up cutting my head or taking out the staples. My head was so numb I just couldn't see where I was cutting and had to go by the feel of where the staples were. The pillow finally dropped so I knew I had done something but I didn't know what.

Crying was an everyday thing for me 24/7 but now in worse pain then I was before and not being able to get my pain pills, I called Tony and told him the situation I was in. I thought he was going to have a heart attack, I told him I wanted the piece of the pillow case that was stuck on one of the staples, off right then. He told me not to do anything but he would be home in 5 minutes. I think it took him 4 minutes.

When he got home he made sure I was okay and then looked at the situation at hand. I told him that I wanted him to pull all the staples out of my head; he gave me that dumb founded look. "What do you want me to do?" I looked at him and told him what I wanted, but more important that because the staples were too big to be pulled out with tweezers, he needed a plier to pull them out. I think by this time he must have thought, "She finally went off the deep end." Somehow I talked him into doing one staple, "Ouch!" But one was enough for him.

He then took me to the doctor's office and told the receptionist what was going on. The look on her face said, "This is an emergency, this patient wants to pull staples out of her head where she had brain surgery and her husband is next to her helpless not knowing what to do without getting into a fight with her. " I got in to see the Doctor right away. I felt bad because every time I went someplace in an emergency and they took me in right away, I felt bad for the patients that were also waiting for their appointment. They looked at me like, "take this lady and do what needs to be done."

This was not my regular doctor and I had been scheduled at a later date to have my staples taken out; at that point in time I think everyone in my life thought that the brain surgery had done something to me because I was doing some crazy stuff. At first the doctor refused to pull the staples out and told me I had to wait till it was time. I told him I didn't have time and the time was now I also told him if he didn't do it I was going to have my husband pull out all of the staples with the pliers and if Tony didn't do it I would do it myself. So reluctantly the doctor took the remaining 24 staples out, but he wasn't too happy about it.

I had just enough time to get home after that incident and take a break to wipe my tears and off to my next appointment for a nerve test. My hands were both hurting, my head was hurting from having the 25 staples pulled out of my head, and I was rushing to go somewhere that I didn't want to go. Nerve tests are very painful and when you have chronic pain like me "and then to top it off this brain surgery,) physically and psychologically those types of tests can be intimidating.

My husband sat and watched as I was given the test and of course I just cried and cried; I thought I had no more tears to give. Tony came to the table and told me to hold his hand. He thought I was going to break his hand because I was squeezing so hard. I didn't think anyone could cry as much as I had.

In April of 1998 I was sent to an orthopedic for consultation and get some test done on my right hand because I was still having constant pain. I was told I needed to have a carpal tunnel surgery done on that hand, I felt sick inside, another surgery. That meant more pills, more appointments. On May 4, 1998 about 5 weeks after I had my stitches out from the brain surgery I was back in the surgery room.

Beside the pain pills I was given other pills for everything else. I continued to get shots for pain from my doctor and when I couldn't get a hold of him I ended up in the emergency room. I think they had a bed with my name on it. It was always you're back again, can't the Doctors do anything? Couple weeks after my hand surgery my husband felt I needed to go to Hawaii to see my family. I knew my mother was constantly worrying about me and needed to see me and that I was okay. I wanted to go but I didn't. I did not want my family to see me the way I was. Tony finally talked me into going and I got the doctors permission to go on the trip. The plane ride was so uncomfortable.

I wore a hat on my head, my right hand was in a sling and I was loaded down with pain pills. I wanted to reassure my family that I was fine and just needed to recuperate. I was happy to see everybody but I was on so many pills and couldn't do anything. One day we all sat down to eat and I was fine but in a couple of minutes broke out in hives. I had these big old welts all over me and I panicked, well once again I ended up at the emergency room in Hawaii, at the closes hospital near the town where my mom lived. Lucky for me one of my sisters worked at this hospital. When I got there she was already at work but was waiting in the emergency room for me.

When I got back to my Moms, I told my family that my vacation would be cut short. I would catch the first flight back to California that I could find, but they understood. I can still picture my Mom sitting in the chair just so sad and crying because of the situation. The plane ride back to California was miserable between the numbness of my head, my hand in a sling because of the carpal tunnel surgery and now I had this horrible itching from these hives from something that I had, later as I was trying to think what I had eaten, it came down to Salmon patties.

For almost a year and a half the left side of my head was so numb, even till today I still get a numbness and pain from surgery. I live with a constant fear that the chips that were implanted in my brain will move and I will be back in the hospital. Anyway I was really miserable because I had lost most of my long hair. The right side of my body also continued to be in pain. Whenever I opened my eyes all I ever saw was drugs, a needle ready to be injected in me, or the toilet bowl as I would throw up. It was my "hell on earth".

As days, weeks, months went by and no comfort was coming my way, I started blaming God for all my misfortunes. Why God? Why are you doing this to me? What have I done in my life to deserve this? Why am I going through so much pain and suffering? I had it with everything. I was so depressed, as far as I was concern I was the loneliest person in the world. How do you paint lonely?

All my life I had so much family and friends around, all I had to do was pick up the phone and make a call. Everyone goes through a point in their life where they start questioning things. At this point in my life, the questions were never ending, the answers never there. The loneness to follow was so loud it was deafening.

CHAPTER FOUR
OPENING THE GATES OF HELL

"Then Jesus said to him, "Away with you, Satan!
For it is written, 'You shall worship the Lord
your God, and Him only you shall serve."
Mathew 4:10

When I first decided to write this book I prayed to God to guide me in my writings. Before I wrote each chapter, I prayed that God would guide me in whatever I penned. As I began to write and tell my story, sitting and inputting information into the computer, I found it easier to do. The first three chapters seemed to just flow as if God was reading my life story to me and all I had to do was input this information into the computer. I couldn't input fast enough for all the data that was stored in my head. At times I wanted to give up, but God was my guide and He knew He would be there for me, because there is no problem so great he can't see me through.

When it came to the chapter I wanted to write called, "Opening the Gates of Hell" all of a sudden I couldn't write. There were so many things to say but no words would come to mind. It was like my mind had gone blank. When I sat to input the information into the computer, even the computer was giving me a hard time; my paper was getting jammed in the printer and it was getting frustrating. One month went by, then two months and I kept praying to God to please tell me what was going on and what to do. Finally, I decided I was going to stop writing my book altogether. I figured when the time was right God would speak to me and tell me the reason why I was having such a difficult time writing this chapter. God knew I would have an open mind as to what He would say.

I have a very wise husband there is no doubt in my mind. When I first met him in 1966, I knew we had nothing in common yet we just connected with each other. I know now God specifically put him on my tiny little island at the right time and at the right place so that we would connect with each other.

It was a time that I called "a time of love and war." The war in Vietnam was raging on and my husband who was my boyfriend at the time was in the United States Marine Corps. He was stationed at the Kaneohe Marine Corps base and was on his way to Vietnam. Hawaii was just a stopover before going to South East Asia. For Tony and for me this stop over would change our lives forever.

As I started to write my book, I would finish a page and have Tony read it or a thought would come to mind and I would ask for his input. I have a lot of respect for whatever input he has to say whether it is something I agree with or not. The one thing he does not like to talk about is my conversion back to my relationship with God and my return to the Seventh Day Adventist church; for the simple fact that he lived everything with me and saw what the Devil can do.

It is bad enough that he went through hell when he was a "combat Marine" in Vietnam, and now over many years later he was going through another time in hell with his wife, or as I refer to this period in my life as "hell on earth." To relieve everything again and again even though it is in writing is not a pretty picture for him and for me it becomes like a recurring dream or video that plays over and over. There are things that he witnessed that I don't remember; things that he won't talk about. For him it was a sad time in his life, to see his wife go through what she went though.

When it comes to the spiritual warfare I had with the devil, my husband was seeing and hearing what was happening to me on the outside. I was seeing, hearing, and feeling what was going on the inside of my mind. No one, not even my husband will ever understand or be a part of what happened to me on the inside. When I say I have come face to face with the devil; I have and I have been to the pits of hell! When I say I have come face to face with God Himself and have seen the Glory of Heaven and the Father, I have. My husband is the only one that truly knows what happened and only saw what God allowed him to witness and see.

Now getting back to my story, I usually tell Tony everything, but for some reason I couldn't tell him the problem I was truly having writing this chapter called "Opening the Gates of Hell." He would say and how is your writing coming along? Is your book finish? If you had seen how fast I wrote the previous chapters, you would understand why he asked me those questions.

One day I asked him to read one of the pages that I had written on this specific Chapter and wanted his input. He turned to me and said, "You don't need to write all of that in your book." I told him why? His answer was very simple Why give the devil so much time in your writing? He said the less you write about the devil the better.

There was so much that I could have written about my encounter with the devil in this chapter but I choose not to. After praying about it I decided there was a reason God put me on hold during my writings. God wanted me to witness Lucifer the Anointed Cherub, Gods divine favor. Lucifer was created perfect in all his ways, but wickedness was found in him. How could I truly understand Gods love if I had nothing to compare it with?

God wanted me to witness the love of God which is powerful and greater than anything that Satan could and will ever do. I knew God in his infinite love and mercy would guide me and give me enough words to pen to get my point across to my reading audiences without lingering on and on; giving Satan his moment of glory was not what I wanted to do. I was afraid to write anything negative about Satan for I was afraid what unknown situation I would have to encounter during my writing and after. Surely Satan had his hold over me, spiritually, mentally and physically. God allowed Satan to take me to the pits of hell to see if I was ready to come back to Him. During my spiritual warfare with the devil, you must understand everything that was happening to me or anything I was saying was not of my choosing.

My time frame isn't clear but I would say in this instant it must have been in the early morning hours about 1 or 2 in the morning. Time is not an issue here, what happened is.

As I sat on the couch in my living room broken and torn feeling rejected from anything and everything, I looked around me and could not place myself in my living room, everything looked familiar but nothing looked familiar. In my mind I wasn't sure who I was or where I was. Out of nowhere I saw my husband, but he wasn't my husband. I looked at him wondering who this person was. This unknown person was on my telephone talking to someone. As I sat there and listened his voice began to change. The sound that I heard was not a familiar sound it had a deep and high pitch sound at the same time. I began to get scared and I asked him who he was and who he was calling. I do not recall what he said although I could see his mouth moving. In my mind he was calling the devil.

Somewhere in this time frame I than thought I heard him say, I am talking to your son, but all I could hear was I am talking to your Satan. I remember yelling at my husband and saying, why are you talking to the devil? Why are you talking to the devil? Crying and angry I could not believe that my husband had gone so far as to call the devil, Satan the evil one.

My husband at that time was about 255 or 260 pounds, he is pretty well built and very strong in comparison to me. Because of his height, his weight is in one mass. You must remember that in January of 1998 I had a tumor removed on the right side wall chest. In May of 1998 I had a carpal tunnel surgery on my right hand. Then in March of 1999 I had another carpal tunnel surgery done on my right hand that extended down to my wrist.

I had been told a year or so ago that because of the surgeries, the nerves in my right arm had been damaged and I would never have the use of my right hand again. My hand was so withered and useless. So that a person can understand the situation, there was no way I could defend myself. Physically I could not hurt anyone. At this point in time I had no strength, and no power. I was just helpless physically, mentally and spiritually.

Now for some reason I was completely confused. My mind had gone completely berserk and I thought my husband was the devil himself. I screamed and shouted, "You are the devil, you are the devil, and you are Satan himself"! Why are you doing this to me, why? I was crying now, tears flowing; there was no way of stopping. Through the tears and pain I knew that somewhere out there my husband was there for me. I couldn't see him, I couldn't hear him, but I could feel his presence. I didn't want to lose touch with him or I would have lost touch with reality never returning back to normal.

I yelled at him who I then thought was Satan, You are Satan! You are Satan! Why are you doing this to me, why? I remembered a voice that kept saying, I am not Satan, I am not the devil, and I am your husband. In my confused mind this was not my husband. I couldn't see him. God! Where are you I cried out? I could feel myself and hear myself saying God, my God why have you forsaken me? My husband came to me and I grabbed the phone out of his hand, he was not my husband, than who was he? Thinking I was going to hit him, Tony came at me and he went to grab the phone out of my hand. With my right hand, the hand that had no power, the hand that had no strength, the hand that was withered, with one fast and swift shove with the palm of my right hand I hit my husband's chest and he went flying across our living room floor. I could see the look on his face and now he knew this could not be his wife.

I was not in control then or of what was happening, I felt helpless to the situation. My husband knew then that he was not dealing with his wife but that some super natural power had gotten a hold of me and my mind, the master of the world of darkness, the devil, Satan himself. As soon as he fell he came up real quick but in that short time frame, when he got to me I had the telephone cord wrapped around my neck three times and was chocking myself to death. In my sick mind I thought I was chocking my husband who at that time I thought was Satan.

My husband tried to get the cord off of me so I wouldn't choke myself to death. He said the strength that I had even he could not believe how he had to wrestle with me to take the cord away. It frightens him to think that all the illness and surgeries that I had to encounter and here he had to fight someone who had the power and strength that I had. Finally, he had to literally sit on me to take the cord out of the grip of my hand. All he knew was that if he did not get the cord off of me I would have chocked myself to death. Tony was praying and crying out all the time to God to help him and with Gods' love and grace He did.

It was more evident now that Tony was truly dealing with Satan and that never in all his life was he asking and pleading for Gods help, more than he had ever asked before. My husband is a true believer in prayer, and he never did pray as hard as he had ever done then in that time frame that he had to deal with the devil. Satan knew than that spiritually I had completely lost it. I was an easy prey to take over; Satan also knew that my husband's faith in God was strong, very strong. Would my husband and his faith in God and his belief that God is there in the good times as well as the bad times be strong enough for the two of us. After what seemed like hours the commotion had settled down. He had called another Adventist couple, and then another friend to come over, they sat in the kitchen afraid to come into the living room, and fearing for their own life they all left scared. Tony was there all alone again with me. Good and evil had finally met in my house.

As I sat in my living room it was now quiet, oh so quiet. My living room now had a deadly scent. An hour or so after the incident with the telephone, I happen to be looking at some pictures on the living room wall. These pictures I had bought them all from China Town in Los Angeles, California. The pictures were made of mother-of-pearl pieces and it is mounted on black wood. The oriental pictures that I had in our living room were about one foot by two or three foot tall; and they were beautiful pictures and that is why I had bought them.

I was now sitting on the living room floor just staring at these pictures. All of a sudden the objects in the pictures began to come to life. The birds and people began to move and I thought how neat. I had two walls with pictures on them. I was fascinated by its movement like the birds were singing to me and the people were talking to me. All of a sudden the room began to spin very slowly like when you ride a merry go round. The room began to go round and round and then it began to pick up speed. It seem like it went from five miles an hour and in a matter of minutes it was going a hundred miles an hour.

What were picture frames now began to change to giant domino blocks; black, black, black, and black everywhere. I couldn't stop the pictures from spinning, I began to yell at my husband to take it down, take it down. He on the other hand kept asking me to take what down. I said, take it down or I am going to die it is going to kill me. By now the room was just spinning faster and faster like a toy top when it goes round and round. Than the four pictures started to merge and it turned into a black coffin. I kept yelling at my husband to take anything that is oriental out of the living room. I don't care what you do with it, take it out they are going to kill me; I am going to die.

By now it was in the early morning of the next day. My husband said he called my son Frank. He lives just around the block from us; and said get over here now I need your help. Within minutes my son was at the house and in record time they instantaneously had all the pictures out of the living room and anything that was oriental went out of the house. I was now screaming at my son to take everything. I don't care what you do with it, keep it, throw it away, sell it, I want it out. The whole time I was yelling, I had my face covered, I didn't want to look. I was afraid if I opened my eyes, I would be looking into the eyes of the devil himself, and I felt death all around me.

During that time frame many incidents occurred. I had a

picture of myself on the wall it was 14" x 16". I am in a black and white Chinese outfit and the picture was taken from the waist up. I remembered looking at that picture and all of a sudden worms started to come out of my eyes, hundreds of worms, they just kept coming out of my eyes, nose, mouth and ears and they started wrapping themselves around the frame of the picture. Fear gripped my heart and I looked down at our carpet and all of a sudden there was thousands of worms on the floor, and I kept yelling to my husband, get it off of me, get it off of me! They had all slithered down the picture and was there just sucking the life out of me.

Turning my eyes away from the floor I looked to one side of the wall and the wall had turned into a cemetery. I saw all my ancestors that had died years ago, everyone that I had found in my genealogy research become alive. Yelling and screaming at them, I kept crying why, why? My whole wall had turned into a graveyard and all the coffins were open and they were all coming to me. There were faces with no eyes, just circles of white, teeth rotted, mangled hair. It was a horrible sight, but in my mind everything was real. The devil had invaded my house, my life, my heart.

I don't remember too much of anything after that. The next morning things had quieted down. Looking around my living room there were holes in the wall where my son had just ripped the pictures off. Within that week I went through my house and most of my oriental items that I found I gave it all away. Why those specific items I don't know. The power of Satan and his demons the fallen angels of God was so unbelievable real, and I just couldn't understand why all of this was happening to me. What had this brain surgery done to my life and would I ever live a normal life after this? Where was God?

God in his love and infinite mercy was with Tony and me the whole time. It was the greatest struggle between good and evil. I do not want to give Satan any more time then he has already taken away from me. I don't want to go on and on and write about what he can and will do to get a person to follow him.

Like a picture that continues to be painted color by color, this chapters color is black, black, black, it is a deep black and unless you have seen the devil himself I hope no one ever sees him. I thank God that He is always with me as I have had to know what deep black, black, black, deep black is like, because of the horrible things that happened, seen and unseen, written and unwritten. Ever since I was a little girl I had seen my mother go through hardships but she always had peace among herself. She taught me about Gods love in so many ways and never turned away even in times of trouble. Her love of God that she would instill in me would bring me through this spiritual warfare. God knew that the one person I counted on to be always there was my mother.

I remember telling my mother about the book and what had happened to me. I said, "Mama when all this was going on I would look down and my arms looked like yours", and she said, "Noe, they were, I was always and will always be there with you", even when I am gone, all you have to do is ask, and God will be there. God knows what is in your heart. Of course my mom is gone physically, but she is always there with me. When I look at pictures of my Mom through her I see a loving God, for God is truly loved and we're His little children.

CHAPTER FIVE
STRETCH FORTH THINE HAND

"Heal me, O Lord, and I shall be healed; Save me
and I shall be saved, For you are my praise".
Jeremiah 17:9

After that long night of darkest hell, the darkness
vanished, God let me see light once again and the pure
white color of His kingdom. As I sat in my living room,
God seemed to walk and talk with me about the past years
of my life. It was as if He was testing me to see if I was
ready to come back to Him. I was so grateful for being
taken out of that horrible darkness and ushered into the
light of His glorious presence again. I pleaded and begged
for His forgiveness and cried out, "If you love me, please
save me!"

God in His wisdom and power didn't give me an answer
at that time. He took my mind back to the beginning of
time when the earth was without form and void; which was
comparable to the void feeling in my brain at that moment.
My poor tortured drug sodden mind was reaching out. I
was trying to find the footprints of Jesus somewhere in
the shifting sands of my wondering years. To me I was
reaching up just trying to touch bottom.

Stored in my mind was the little dream story about a wayward, crippled sinner like me sitting all alone on a sandy beach. Facing a rising tide, suddenly Jesus appeared nearby and I cried out for help. Immediately Jesus stretched forth His hand and lifted me to my feet and led me up the sand beach to safety. But like the footprints in the sand, I could only see one set of tracks and asked Jesus why there was only one set. That's when He informed me, "It is because I have been with you like a crippled child who could not walk I have been carrying you."

As I sat there my mind continued back to Jesus' crucifixion in Jerusalem. I saw Jesus carrying the cross with that cruel crown of thorns on His head. My head ached in sympathy with His because of the staples that had been used on my head for my brain surgery; I had only the weight of my sins on my head Jesus had the weight of the world. I have sinned so many times Jesus is pure and white as snow, but yet they put a crown of thorns on His head.

I watched helplessly as the nails were pounded through His hands at the cross. The pain in my withered hand because of the carpel tunnel ached in sympathy with His and in anguish that surgery had been done to me but someone made a mistake and I should never had that surgery done. But Jesus, He who had healed the sick, now His hands were been nailed with the hate of the world.

In my mind I saw the soldiers thrust the spear into His side and I cringed remembering the flash of hot pain of the surgeon's knife when the tumor was removed from my side. Was I trying to make a comparison to Jesus? NEVER! But God was letting me see why I must return to Him, how His love would carry me through, no matter what.

Suddenly all those years of going to church not truly understanding the crucifixion of Jesus and his death; now His suffering and death on the cross was made clear to me. Christ had paid for all my rebellious "wondering years" long before I was ever born. Now I understood why I was allowed to suffer all the things I did. I had to understand what my waywardness cost God and His son Jesus before they could offer me a second chance.

It was then that Jesus performed His first miracle for me. I knew He was inviting this poor lost sheep, to return home to Him. In my mind I heard Him say, "Stretch forth thine hand" and I did. He touched me and the pain in my withered hand immediately stopped. I knew then that God was slowly coming back into my life but there was more, so much more I needed.

As I talked to God I asked Him to give me peace in my life. I needed a sign to let me know that my walk with Him was a reality. At that time I needed to be delivered from all the prescription drugs that I had been taken. I knew I would need some and thank God for what I did have; but I had so much, prescription after prescription, bottles and bottles of pills.

There was so much evil in my life the day before. I asked God, please answer my prayers. I know God answer people in different ways. God would answer my prayers through a little piece of paper. Tony had tried to get a hold of different Pastors to come over the night before and could not believe that they all had excuses why they couldn't come. He was getting so discouraged and desperate. It was as if the devil had put a spell on these Pastors. Finally he got in contact with a Pastor that we both knew years ago when we were first married, we had gone to his church. He wasn't an Adventist minister but he told Tony that he would come. In the wee hours of the night this Pastor and his assistant did come. Tony told me who was coming and I remembered the Pastor so many years ago, at that time I don't remember too much of what or why that Pastor was there, except that Tony had called him and he had responded. But he was not the one.

Later that morning while rummaging through a desk drawer my husband found a piece of paper which had slipped to the back of a specific draw many years ago. He called the number and God was working in my behalf now and Tony got hold of this Seventh Day Adventist Pastor. He was a former missionary to Hawaii who was now retired. When Tony told him what had happened he agreed to come and help me at that late hour. Once again the hour was not the time of the day, but the time of need.

Early the next morning while waiting in my living room for this pastor, I was staring at the television although it wasn't on. Suddenly my tormentor of so many years decided to reveal himself to me in person again and I could feel the presence of fear, I closed my eyes but it didn't matter. Before The devil, Satan himself could enter my space or cause me anymore fear or pain, my husband announced, the Pastor is here. I turned from the apparition as I searched for the Pastor through the disheveled hair hanging over my face from my encounter with the devil. Not saying anything to the Pastor, I looked at him and he looked at me and quoted the text of Philippians 4:7, "and the peace of God which passeth all understanding shall keep your hearts and minds through Jesus Christ."

All of a sudden there was peace, and I could think clearly. Although he had told me the Pastors name, I didn't remember it. I proceeded to tell the Pastor what had happened and the Pastor turned to talk to my husband to give him encouragement through the ordeal that Tony was going through. I listened as they talked and the Pastor was describing my vision that I had had the day before. I was amazed, how could this Pastor tell my husband something I hadn't told him.

In the vision that I had, I could see Satan as he was before he became who he was. I saw a being that was pure and such beauty and glowing and he had many angels that followed him. As time went on his beauty and glory began to turn because of jealousy until I saw a creature that I could not describe. When Satan left there were other angels there that would follow him wherever he went. When Satan fell so did 1/3 of the angels.

In my vision as these angels roamed the earth they led many lambs of God astray. I was one of those lambs. In my quest for seeking out good versus bad and pleading with God to help me, He did by sending someone that truly loved the Lord and my prayers would be answered.

God was starting a complete healing process in my life in every way. I still needed something that I could see physically with my own eye that would tell me this is truly the Pastor that God had sent. There was something about this Pastor that had a calming effect on me, so I started to listen to him. We started to talk, he told me a little about himself. He was a Seventh Day Adventist Pastor and he mentioned that he had pastored in Hawaii. Of course that caught my attention and as we spoke I realized that he knew people from Hawaii that I knew; but I still needed more.

I proceeded to tell the pastor about Jesus and the footprints in the sand and how I felt He had been carrying me all the time. And then that "something" appeared. It was like God was telling me, if you seek Me you will find Me. The Pastor began to smile and pointed to his tie. As I looked at it, it was blue with little footprints and in the back of the tie was the words "footprints in the sand." The Pastor, Tony and I were surprise because of what his tie represented. To me that was Gods physical way of telling me, I have sent you a Man of God.

The author Francine and Pastor Varner Leggitt and his wife.
The Pastor sent from God.

Let me forward a little bit in my story. I had wanted so much to get ahold of Pastor Leggitt, for he was the Pastor that God had sent me. I have not seen the Pastor since our last meeting where I had given my testimony and sang years ago. I prayed that God would send me Pastor Leggitt so that I could let him read my manual scrip, since he was such an important person in my story of healing. This particular Sabbath, Tony asked me if I was going to church, I told him right now the time is not right for me, I'm still so lost and trying to find my way. When Tony came home from church he said you're not going to believe this, I said what and he handed me this phone number. I looked at him and said, well whose number is it? Pastor Leggitt, once again God had answered my prayer, once again He knew that even though I was still trying to find my way, He was going to show me the way. Like the little piece of paper Tony found years ago in searching for the right pastor once again a little piece of paper this time handed to me. I truly believe God sent Pastor Leggitt to me in my time of need.

Going back to my story, I hated looking into the mirror because what I saw looking back at me was horrible. I stopped calling family and friends and soon would become more of a hermit except to my sons and their families. There were more blood test to come and I thought how much more blood can they get out of me? In my head anyone who took blood from me was vampire's just draining, and draining blood from me sucking the life out of me and I could not fight back.

Now I knew God was in my life again, in reality He had never left me. I was the one that had closed the door. I waited to see if as the days went by, Satan would continue to taunt and harass me and He did. Through my continuing struggle my Heavenly Father was still watching over me. Yes I had prayed and prayed but to me no answer came, and

I grew weak in my faith. I knew God wouldn't leave me, He just wanted me to hold on, He wanted me to see what a miracle was like. He was working for me all the time.

In our lives we get so busy with everything we truly forget that God is always on our side all we have to do is call upon Him and He will hear our pleading and answer our call.

While working on my book, the Devil caused so many interferences and problems. Anyone can tell me it was just your imagination. But I know it wasn't, for instance every time I wrote something about Satan, for some reason when I was done what I had just inputted disappeared from the screen. Devil, Satan himself continued to put things in my mind that would confuse me so that at times I would input words that made no sense.

I was struggling with my writing I would talk to God as I wrote to help me get my point across to whoever would read my book. How could I show people the love of God if I couldn't make sense as to what I was writing? Then my hands would get so numb that I was struggling just to input my data. I thought Lord, am I supposed to write this book on my own? I just cannot do it! I have had to struggle through so many dark days and night just trying to get a page or two written. Was it really worth it?

Then Satan would say to me, "Follow me, and I will make sure you do not have to struggle, I will give you the right words to say." My mind was being contaminated by evil thoughts. Like a bonsai tree whose growth is limited so was my mind and what I was trying to do.

Like a palette that has so many different colors, colors that can bring ones painting to life on the canvas, I wanted the same colors, I wanted to bring life to my story on a sheet of paper. It seems like I had so much interference in my thoughts, so many doubts as I continued to write. Was my mind going to be strong enough to continue writing this book? At times my hands would be numb and I couldn't feel anything as I typed.

Frustrated I would sit and cry, angry at everything that was happening in my life, negativities invading my thoughts. But through God's understanding I realize that whatever stumbling block that was before me I could overcome. I would find the right words so that whoever read my book would understand the love of God and His forgiveness.

My computer kept messing up, so finally I just couldn't handle it and told Tony, "I need to get a new computer." He said, "Okay." He felt I had had mine for a number of years, so we went ahead and obtain a new computer and printer. But whenever I worked on my book and inputted anything about Satan my computer jammed up. I remember doing a whole chapter on this subject and as I sat looking at the screen everything just disappeared. I now knew that Satan was still trying to interfere with my writing, my mind and my life.

So before I inputted anything I asked God to please help me get my point across, and please don't let my computer down on me. I didn't want to be doing what I was doing, but I needed to do this book. I wanted people to see that there are miracles all around us, that if we ask Jesus to help us, He will be there in the good times and the bad times. I knew my faith in God would bring me through the storm.

My pallet of colors began to come back to life and as I looked to see what color I would need, I could see the out stretched hands and knew that whatever color I would use would be the right one. Like the paint with many colors, I would be given the right words to say to get my point across.

Thank you Lord, for getting me this far in my book, that whatever lays in front of me now will be nothing as to what you will present to me in the future. Whatever cross I have to bear is nothing compared to that cross on Calvary where my Savior died for me.

CHAPTER SIX
SPINNING OUT OF CONTROL
MENTAL HOSPITALS

"Blessed *are* the poor in spirit, for theirs is the
kingdom of heaven. Blessed are those who mourn,
for they shall be comforted."
Mathew 5:3,4

After my conversion back to God I thought that I
would not have any more suffering or crisis in my life. Two
days later I woke up and I was bleeding, I thought the bleeding
would stop but I would continue to bleed. Within the next
15 hours I would bleed heavily, then I started hemorrhaging,
profuse bleeding. I told Tony I needed to get to the medical
facility near our house. When I got there they took me in
right away when they realized the situation.

I hate going to any kind of medical facility or emergency
and seeing the room filled with people and the medical
facility or emergency room take you in right away to see
the Doctor.   I know what it is to be waiting for hours, but
thank God those that were waiting saw the seriousness of
what was happening; they all had this look on their face
like she needs them more than we do

The nurses and doctors at the medical facility tried
everything they could to stop the bleeding but to no avail.

They just looked helpless and didn't know what to do except tell me they were calling an ambulance to take me to the emergency room at another hospital. My husband said he would take me because he could get me there faster than they could. He helped me in the car and we went speeding to the hospital. I was so afraid he was going to get a ticket. By the time we got there and went into the emergency room big chucks of blood like liver was gushing out of my body. Tony told me later, even when he was in Vietnam he hadn't seen as much blood as that night in the emergency room with me. Till today he still says it was unbelievable that I am still here.

With all that was going on what was to happen next left me in a state of confusion. I was on the bed in the emergency room and the medical personal had covered me with a white sheet and said they would be back. I waited and waited but not a single nurse or doctor came in. I could feel the blood was just oozing out of me, but in all that was going on I wasn't panicking. A nurse finally comes in and I told her I was bleeding heavily but she paid no attention.

While I'm telling the nurse what is going on with me another nurse comes in and wants to get a blood test. I'm looking at them like are you crazy. They kept poking and poking me and trying to get something but was having no luck at all. I said you're not going to get any blood from me that way.

I was just so disgusted with everything and said something like, if you want blood just look under the sheet and you can have as much as you want. They thought I was being sarcastic, finally one of the nurses decided to look under the sheet, when she looked at me her face turned white. I thought "great she is going to pass out". She ran out of the room so fast and in no time was back with another nurse or doctor. I can't remember what they gave me. They said that would stop the bleeding and of course it didn't, I kept bleeding and bleeding. Tony was so disgusted that he started grabbing their clean white towels and ended up using about 14 heavy duty towels to clean up the mess.

Finally, the bleeding did stop and since no one was there I told Tony take me home. I had been there all night and just wanted to get home. We had already told one of the nurses that I wanted to leave. She said she would get the Doctors okay, but like always I waited and waited and finally I told Tony I've had it let's go. As we were leaving a nurse passed by me and I told her; "by the way I kind of left the room a mess". She said, okay we'll send someone in to clean it. I pity the person that had to do that.

The following Friday I had some kind of attack. I couldn't breathe and it seemed like my heart was pumping and going a hundred miles an hour. Every-thing inside of me was going chaotic. After that I don't remember anything, one minute I was at home, the next minute I was in the emergency room. It seems the days were turning into weeks and the weeks into months, there were so many heartaches going on in my house. I felt completely useless like I shouldn't be here and Tony was doing everything he could to keep things going. I was like a zombie wondering around in a daze and thinking why is all of this happening to me to me. Tony and I had a wonderful marriage. We were always there for our boys and who ever needed our help. Nothing seemed to make sense as far as I was concerned.

One day I had a call from the Pastor Legitt who had come to my rescue. The Pastor is the one who had the tie with the footprints in the sand. He wanted to talk to me and asked me if I would go with him to different churches within our denomination and give my testimony and sing. I was kind of hesitating, I didn't know if I would be able to give a testimony or sing and then what song would I sing. I called my Mom to tell her what the Pastor wanted me to do. She thought it was a good idea and it would let people know about the love of God.

So we started going to different churches. After each testimony I would conclude with singing the song "Stretch Forth Thine Hand" (I would change some of the wording to fit my situation) and "I Believe in a Hill Called Mt. Calvary." Then one day at home I started to say something and I couldn't hear myself, I couldn't talk. As I was preparing to go to the next church on my list and give my testimony, it was as if the devil had cut my tongue out and I couldn't talk. I knew that Satan had come back into my life again. I would beg and plead with God to show me the way to let me know what was going on. When I got my voice back I called the Pastor and told him that I would not be doing anymore testimony.

Now the bleeding that had stopped had come back again. I was bleeding daily and losing weight. I went to the doctor and he told me I needed to have a D and C surgery. This is a procedure to scrape and collect the tissue (endometrium) from inside the uterus. It's a common surgery, I mean all surgery has their risks but it's not like the brain surgery that I had. I figured he was the Doctor.

So a date was set; but before the date he called me in once again. He told me that I needed to have a hysterectomy. Again I saw no problem at this point. If this was going to stop the bleeding and help me with the medical problems I was having then go ahead and do the surgery. His only concern was that I was still recuperating from my other surgery and how mentally I would be able to handle it. I told him it seems like both surgeries I was to have were normal procedures and so a date was set. I was told I would be in the hospital for a couple of days.

Hospitals, emergency rooms, doctor offices, etc. they were like second homes to me. Another surgery just meant more work for Tony and more misery for me. So once again it was surgery time. After the surgery and out of the recovery room I was now in my own hospital room. My Gynecologist came in and the look on his face told me something was wrong. He asked me how I was feeling and I told him tired but okay. What he told me next shocked my husband and me. He said while doing the hysterectomy, which is an operation to remove a woman's uterus, he found a tumor the size of a baby's head growing on my uterus. He said that all the problems I had with my bleeding and cramps were due to the tumor.

As he was explaining to me when he was doing the D and C he had no choice of doing just a normal hysterectomy he had to do a radical hysterectomy; then he proceeded to tell me about it. I was hearing him but I wasn't hearing him. It was like I needed some kind of proof he in turn must have been reading my mind. He said I didn't think you would believe me so we had pictures taken of the tumor to show you how big it was, also another picture with the tumor cut in half to show you there was no cancer. Tony and I both looked at the pictures in dismay. How a tumor could get so big and none of the Doctors I went to, or x-rays showed this tumor was just strange. The pathways of my life just seemed to be going in so many different directions. I began to feel like Satan was doing everything in his power mentally and physically to take me down.

I finally was out of the hospital and started to feel a little better, I was on my way to recovery, I still had a lot of problems but I tried real hard to focus on the good things in life and how God had brought Tony into my life. One day I stood up to get something and my knee gave out on me. The pain that shot through me scared me a little. I hated to tell Tony about it or my doctor. I had an appointment and when the doctor was examining me he touched my knee and I almost went through the roof.

I finally had to tell him about my knee and the pain I was having. A little over a month from my D and C and hysterectomy surgery I had to have a knee arthroscopic surgery. Even though in this kind of surgery you use less anesthetic, less cutting and less recovery time, the surgeon still has to have a very thorough examination of the cause of knee injury or pain.

Several years earlier I had a similar knee surgery. I had gone to a church function and was playing volleyball and when I went down to hit the ball I fell on my knee. I went home that night and although my knee was sore I didn't think anything of it until the next day when I got up in pain and my knee had swelled three times its normal size. So now I had this procedure on the same knee. At times it seems like my knee cap is floating. Okay so now I would have instability knee problems. For the next couple of weeks I was off my feet and was using crutches. Would it never end?

The holidays were now here and I was getting depressed because of what was happening to me. I was having headaches and it scared me because if the chips they had put in my head moved the Doctors told me they would have to go in and fix it. Even though I had been reassured by the Surgeon that the chips would not move there is not a 100% guarantee that it won't.

My right hand was constantly having a tingling feeling and I thought I was going to have more problems with my hand. The medical aids that were given to me to help me were no help. The crutches that were given me were of no use because of the surgery I had under my arm. I was given some kind of contraption to put around my neck so that it would help with the back problems that I was having; but because of my brain surgery it hurt when I tried to use it and almost hung myself because I couldn't get it off fast enough. The tears, the pain, the loneliness never stop and the year 2000 ended with more problems. But the biggest problem that I would ever encounter lay ahead of me.

By the beginning of 2001 I was going into a deep depression. I would do absolutely nothing, just sit and stare into space. Going back and forth to my Doctor he began to see the changes in me, and felt that there was no other alternative but to put in a mental hospital and see what would happen. I was there for three weeks. While there I would sit and watch the other patients, I couldn't believe that I was one of them, that my life had taken such a turn.

Where was my God? I now was just another statistic in a mental hospital that dealt with so many patients like me.

As I began to talk to the different patients they let me into their world because I was now one of them, I couldn't believe it. Had Satan just taken me and thrown me into the lion's den?   God can you hear me? I began to talk to the other patients and they came from all walks of life, having all kinds of jobs.   There were patients in there that had Master Degrees. I also talked to a patient that was a nurse and asked her how can you end up in a place like this? She told me that she became a nurse to help people, to stop their hurting and misery. She couldn't do what she had wanted to do to help them ecause it just depressed her and she was now one of them.

Within the next 5 months I would end up in the mental hospital several times. I just couldn't get out of this depression. My husband was very concerned. He always has been concerned and felt I should go to Hawaii to see my family. So it was back to Hawaii but because of my knee surgery there wasn't much I could do. So I just recuperated there for a while. When I got back to California things seem to be going fine for a while.

It was the middle of April 2001, my knees continued to bother me and I couldn't get out of my depression mood. I thought mentally I was fine but I wasn't. The pain that was going through my body was never ending, like I said, drugs, to get up, drugs to go to sleep, drugs for pain and it went on and on. One day in a 6 hour time frame I took 21 Tylenol with Codeine #4 but the pain never subsided. My life seemed to be spinning out of control. I started playing Doctor and would try one pill with another, seeing what it would do. Because of the amount of Doctors I had, I also had a lot of pills.

There are no tomorrows as far as I was concerned. Life for me so far had been challenging. I lived in a world of pain and prescription pills. When I was alone the tears wouldn't stop, the pain wouldn't go away, and I hated and I hated and I hated everything. I would talk to Satan and cry to God, or talk to God and cry to Satan. My world was upside down and I didn't know who to turn to. When I was a child my Mother had always told me to turn to God, but in my mind I didn't know who God was. Was God the Devil or was the Devil God? My days turned into nights, and nights into days, and then I didn't know the difference between AM and PM, I hated myself. At this point in time without my health I felt I had nothing left. I learned how to do things so that everyone around me thought I was fine and if I wasn't, well it was all the medication I was taking, all the surgeries I had. I didn't need excuses for anything, if you knew me you would have done anything I asked just so you would be the one to stop the pain, to stop the crying, just to bring a smile back on my face.

One night I couldn't sleep; which was one of many, long before the first ray of sun proclaimed yet another brilliant day; I laid awake thinking of my life, the past, the present and the future. Rest was out of the question for me. It wasn't a matter of how much rest I would get but rather how much pain would elude me. I had disrupted my family's life. I didn't know what my boys were thinking at the time. I felt I had forced my husband to endure things that he shouldn't have had to. I had left him between a rock and a hard stone because I didn't want people to find out what my life was really like. He would get phone calls and make excuses for me.

The music for me had stopped. My eyes were open but they couldn't see, my ears could hear but it heard nothing. The pulse of my soul was not beating it was just a silent echo and a beat away from nowhere. My commitment to my marriage was to be a good wife not a useless one. I had no control of my life. I couldn't make decisions, and little things overwhelmed me, I was now a useless wife and mother as far as I was concern.

Every morning I got up, I would stare vacantly into space, for somewhere in space was the Devil or my God. At this point I couldn't tell the difference. Tony hated going to work because he didn't want me left alone. I would argue with him about him wanting to bring someone else into the home to be with me. In my mind if he brought anyone in and I didn't want them, I was going to make their life so miserable that they would never come back again. Now alone it seemed depression was taking over my life, and I didn't know how to stop it. I hated all the pills I was taking with a passion. Just to see me smile my husband would have done anything.

My mind would go back to the stormy night when my husband could not help me anymore and he looked at me crying because he was in such a desperate and helpless situation. I would look at him and he was just crying from his heart. Talk about a bleeding heart, his was bleeding but the blood was coming out of me. He had always been there for me, and it made me sad to think of all the things I was putting him through. And all the time I would just stare vacantly into space. Then the tears stopped, no more crying, no more, no more caring about anything.

Then I was a person that had nothing left at least in my mind I had nothing left, just a broken body, a broken spirit and a broken mind, and Satan took over, I wanted to commit suicide. I remember taking a razor blade; but I also remembered my husband saying how hurt he would be if anything happened to me. This particular morning I was just so desperate, I was in a corner with nowhere to turn because every place to turn brought me pain. Finally crying I called Tony at work I told him in so many words what was on my mind. It seems like before I got off of the phone he was home. Thank God my mind at this point in time could not think fast enough.

When he got home, he just didn't know what to say, he wasn't mad but he felt so helpless, and it was worse because for me there was no hope and we sat down and had a long talk. I realized now that to stay home by myself was not possible. He called my Doctor and explained the situation. After he hung the phone up he stated that the best thing to do was to go to a place where I could be helped, of course I didn't care where I went. I spent the next couple of days in a mental hospital. You could have told me it was a baby hospital or an animal hospital it didn't matter, I didn't care.

In the mental hospital to me it seemed normal to be in a place like that because everyone in there had the same kind of problem one way or another. If you became violent or needed to be by yourself you were put in a room all alone and the rooms would be locked with nothing in except for a bed. At any other time I would have been horrified to think I would be in a place like that, but because of my state of mind this is where I needed to be.

While in the mental hospital, the patients are encouraged to write a daily journal. For me journaling came easy because I love to write although I am not very good at grammar. Sometimes I would write a letter to myself but at the end of the day toss it away. When the Psychiatrist would call me in to talk to me, it all depended on how my day went whether he got an answer from me. If I just sat there and said nothing, he would say, I can't help you if you don't talk. So angrily I would say if you want to know how my day went read what I wrote.

For the most part I wrote poems of my sadness and sorrow. But this would get me through the day, and my Doctors would know how to treat me. I didn't realize poems of anger or suicide would mean more pills, because they didn't know where my mind was at and didn't know what I was going to do next.

In March, 2009 I had a book of poetry published called, "Reflections Into My Soul". The following are some of the poems that are in that book, which I felt was important that I have it republished in this book to show the state of mind that I was in at the time. One never knows where their state of mind is truly at unless they are put into a situation that is beyond their control.

The Journey for me seemed endless. I would cry and cry and I thought there are no more tears, but they kept coming. Tony would take pictures after pictures just hoping one of them would bring a big smile. It would take a long time before it happen.

The Journey Is Long

The journey is long when I think of the past I'm tired of surgeries and pills, how long will they last? What started out as one turned into so many, God forgive me when I took too much "bennies". The road that I travel, the path that I take, split into different directions it's a choice that I make. The journey is long when I look down the road, I see a rough walkway I see a heavy load.

I'm tired I'm hurting, I'm always sick, there's a "time bomb" inside of me, I can hear the silent tick. If there is one thing in life I always held with pride, I am married to the best I am a "Marine Corps" bride. Fame through my fingers a talent some said I had, I guess having all these talents wasn't too bad. When I smelled the flowers or looked at a tree, I remembered the garden I made; it was just for you and me. So when God says it's time to depart remember Honey, I loved you with all of my heart.

Please Let Me Be!

Please, let me be when I cry & tears come down like rain, remember my surgery when it was all about my brain. Please, let me be when my days are dark and dreary, life has not been easy and now I am so tired and weary. Please, let me be even if it's a sunny day, year after year the surgery and pills sucked my life away. Please let me be even if you don't want to see me die, I'll always live in your heart I will never, say Goodbye.

Please let me be, help our sons to understand, I always tried to be the best mother I always extended a hand. Please let me be don't let me down, I got tired of living and tired of hanging around. Please let me be don't shed any tears for me, I had enough and only God could see. Please let me be, think of the past, enjoy the memories and the moments we had a lifetime they will last.

Please let me be, think of my best days when I talked and talked and had so much to say. Please let me be, just listen as I sing, because throughout my life you always let me do my thing. Please let me be I loved you with all of my heart, but the time has come and I must depart. Don't cry and say I wish you were here, I never left you and I will always be near. When you think of me in tears and sorrow, remember what you told me about my tomorrows. Let me rest I'm so tired you see, God said it was my time to go so, please let me be.

I Waited For Death

Just around the corner down by the sea, I walked on the white sand asking God to take me. The day was beautiful the sun shone bright, but my days always seem to run into the nights. I wished for death each time I closed my eyes, hoping and praying this will be the day that I die. Death seems so peaceful, so quiet and serene, not like the fast pace in life where everyone just screams.

The water falls of Hawaii I think of so long ago, makes me want to go to Heaven, Lord please take my soul. Life hasn't always been beautiful and kind, through the years it has played with my mind.

I wished for death I didn't have life left in me, the fire that I once had for living, burned out you see. For every smile, for every laugh look into my soul, there are sad stories, stories that are complicated you know.

Each step I take every day, reminds me of the pain that I have had to pay. A thousand and one tear I did cry, but nobody cared to look inside. I wished for death if only for me, just leave me alone and let me be.

Depression

Depression I know what it's all about, after you talk to me you will have no doubt. I'm not crazy or insane, but only myself to blame. I'm preoccupied with death all the time, and if God called me now I would say take me I don't mind. You may say I'm unreasonable to write this way, that's okay just listen to what I have to say.

Do you know what it's like to be depressed? When you're always trying to do your best? It's something that you cannot foresee, who can predict depression not you or me. Year by year the thoughts crept into my head, I have these thoughts so excuse me when I'm dead. Life became boring I was always preoccupied, death seemed so nice so just let me die.

Depress people can look as healthy as can be, but deep inside there's a violent storm arousing in me. For the thousand tears that flow from my eyes, there's a thousand more tears crying inside. I'm not mentally sick because I think this way; I haven't always been good so that is the price I must pay. Don't look at me I'm not out of my mind, just thoughts of depression all the time,

Don't Pity Me

Don't pity me while I am in there, don't pity me please don't stare. Step into my shoes if only for a day, you really wouldn't know what to say, and I would really understand but if you are my friend just extend your hand.

Where were you when I made the call, I tried so hard not to fall. I don't want your pity just look at me, don't turn your face away I'm hurting can't you see? Suicide, depression, sadness and pain, if it continues it will drive me insane. The thoughts keep going round in my head, like a merry-go-round if it doesn't stop I will be dead!

At nights I can't sleep I'm afraid to close my eyes, I won't get up maybe it's my time to die. Life isn't fair if you cry constantly, when I fall down on my knees I plead with God to set me free. Loads of love from the best, doesn't help if your mind is a mess. Don't make me mad, don't set me on fire, and whatever you do don't call me a liar! When all is said and all is done, when I can smile and see the setting sun, when life's tribulation has set me free, do what you like but don't pity me!

G-U-I-L-T-Y

I feel so guilty so all alone, I don't mean to complain but please let me moan, I haven't decided what to say, just hear me out is it okay? Suspicious thoughts you can find in my head, is anyone listening to me doesn't anyone know what I've said? It seems I'm sorry all the time, I feel humiliated at least that's what's on my mind. Paranoid I'm not but I must face reality or that guilty feeling will eat at me.

I'm a shame that the one I love has to go through this all again, I know in his heart he wonders for my sake when will it end? Emotions inside of me keeps yelling, I want to be free, how many times do I have to face reality? I try to be optimistic not negative and guilty, yet the thoughts that go through my mind thank God their not filthy. The frustration that I feel, the fear in my life, I've tried so hard yet I'm so sorry that I couldn't be a normal wife.

137

I'm cautious but overwhelmed by life are you shocked? Don't be surprised if the next time you see me I'll be boxed. I'm guilty not surprise by the way that I feel, but to many times as I looked back at life, I've felt like a heel. If you walked the path that I traveled down the lonely road you see, stop for a moment and take the time to talk to me.

Rage

I can feel the rage building inside of me like a violent storm descending on the deep blue sea. I can feel the rage coming from within and when it hits it will be quicker than the wind. What is that rage only I can see? What is that rage eating up inside of me? Who robbed me of the freedom in my dreams? Even though it was turmoil it was my scene. The fury and wrath that flows through my brain, tells me somewhere down the road I am going insane. The peace and dream I once desired disappeared in the night like an open fire. Through the tears, cries always embarrassed on my part, so many times it gave me a broken heart. As each day goes by and my memory fades away what sort of memory in my heart will stay?

Will I be hurt because I thought no one was there? Who gives a dam about this whole depression affair? Right now I am unworthy, I look at myself and I feel so dirty. Will the heartache and uncontrollable feeling go away and if it does will it come back another day?

What is in the future I hope it's not like the past because the years in my life have gone by too fast! If this rage silent through it may be erupts one day, will it set me free? My eyes close and I remember the man on the cross, and I think of my God and His tremendous lost. Oh God, if this rage continues in me, my life will be hell so set me free!

My Lonely Teardrop

I found a lonely teardrop and I didn't have to look far, all I did was lift up my eyes and look at the falling star. It's my very lonely teardrop because it stands for one, it's my only lonely teardrop as it fell upon my gun. What is this obsession that is blinding me you see? What is this obsession it's hurting the one I love and me? My very lonely teardrop when it starts it will be like rain, it will pour and hit the ground but I will feel the pain. I wish I could change my outlook on life and hope for the best, but my very lonely teardrop won't give me a rest.

When the world looks at me, they will say, have you succeeded in life? Than my lonely teardrop starts to fall, how can I continue to be a good mother and a good wife? What is success if I'm always in pain? What is success if my teardrop falls like rain? Who will measure whatever I do? Just those around me but some make me look like a fool.

The problem I had I could not share, when I faced people to tell them, they didn't care. If only to say hey, look did I pass the test? Did I do okay I tried my best? But there was always something wrong when they looked at me, always a lonely teardrop they would see. I've measured my life by others remark, I should never have done that all it ever gave was a broken heart. Will I ever learn that the dreams I once had, now the dreams that I hoped for now only makes me sad? I tried to steal some happiness along life's narrow road, and all along life's pathway a lonely teardrop did I hold.

To get to a smile I had to work so hard, life had thrown me a Jokers card. I'm not asking for riches or fame, I just don't want to go insane. I want my lonely teardrop to bring me happiness, I want all the surgery and pills to stop, I just want some rest. Please anyone when you look at me, don't look at my tears I don't know what you will see, look at my heart, look into my soul, but don't look at me like I am empty and cold. I do have a heart I do really care but life dealt me something that now it's so hard to bear. It started as a lonely teardrop as you can see, but forget about the past take the time out to cry and laugh with me.

I'm so Confused

Look at me hiding behind a closed door, life to me just seem to be a bore. I've completed so many things in my life; I've even made it over 30 years as a wife. I wish I could go back to when I was a child, when everything in my life was simple and mild.

I saw through the eyes of an innocent girl and all I could think about was to travel the world. To the hills of Switzerland I could touch the sky; I would never have ever contemplated to die. The decisions I've made through the years you see, was everyone's decisions but never me. When did it begin who even knows why? Maybe it was when my father died.

Who was my guidance God only knows, all my life everyone just told me so. I'm trying so very hard not to complain, but I guess it's better than going insane, I can write & write about life itself, so people can read about it on their bookshelf. I'm so lonely very lonely way deep inside, and all I do is cry and cry. I get so confuse by power and fame and I have learned how to play the game. My story is short but I can make it long as it can be, because I will be the only one telling on me.

Right now I don't know who I should be, do I shift back to a child when I was just three or should I become the person that I am, always getting people out of jams? I could write and write and never complete my life, unless I decided to take it with a knife. I get flashbacks of suicide,

I know how easy it is to take my life and die, suicide I've tried to do it three times before, and it was always behind closed doors.

"Heal me, O Lord, and I shall be healed; Save me,
and I shall be saved, For you arc my praise."
Jeremiah 17:14

It was never my choice to end up in different mental hospitals. In fact I ended up in the mental hospital several times. It was either depression or thoughts of suicide or attempts at it. Am I ashamed of having to be there, I will have to say no, God was always a guide and it showed me that no matter where you are in life, no matter how desperate and depress you are, God will be there and he will never give you more than you can handle.

The year 1998 started off bad for me. In January a tumor removed from my right wall chest, in March 1998 my brain surgery, in May 1998 a carpal tunnel surgery. Towards the end of May and the first week of June, I was in Hawaii visiting my family. When I got back I was always in so much pain. I was constantly feeling sick with the medications I was taking. June had been a hot month; bad heath and medications do not mix. Also because of the amount of medications I was taking, I was always so nauseated or dizzy.

It was at this time, at one of the lowest points in my life I would sit and wonder what the future would be like. This night I had it with my life, I could not see any more tomorrows. I went and got a gun. I decide suicide was the only way out for me. I knew that when a person commits suicide they lose their chance of being a child of God but my options were up. The pain was so unbearable. Anyway who was listening? Was God listening, I had pleaded and pleaded for Him, but I could not find Him Where was my God?

Getting one of the guns we had, I went into our bedroom where my husband was asleep. I quietly told him how sorry I was that life had not been fair to him. As he slept, I also told him he had fought his hell in Vietnam and now he was going through another hell with me.

As I stood there in the bedroom, the street light shone into our bedroom. My husband sleeping happened to turn and thought I was a Viet Cong with a gun without hesitation he got up from his sleep and pushed me down. We struggled with the gun, thank God it didn't go off or it could have killed both of us.

After things settled down, I cried as I told him I was tired of living. He then calmed me down and as always he said he loved me and just didn't know how to help me. I was getting desperate because in my world at that time there was no options for anything. But how long was this going to go on? There was no end in sight. How had my life gone from the best that anyone could want to the worst and would I ever get back what I had before, physically, mentally and spiritually?

People would never understand why I did what I did. People would never understand why I would commit suicide especially believing in God. People would never understand how desperate a person can get when they feel they have nothing left in life. For Tony it would be the worse. Since the day I said I do, life could not have been better. I mean if my life was turning upside down what was this doing to him?

Almost a week had pass and my mind would snap once more. Even as I laid in bed staring vacantly into space, my mind was still working. I was still trying to figure out a way to get rid of myself and the pain that was going through my body. The pain that was messing my head up, the pain that I saw through my eyes as I daily watched my husband go through what he had to; something that no husband should have to do. I had failed once again; I couldn't even take my life with a gun, failure in my life that's all I could see.

Going into the kitchen I got a knife. The whole time fighting with my inner thoughts and knowing that this was not the answer. Yet in some ways I was crying for help and didn't know how to tell anyone. I went into the bedroom to tell Tony goodbye. He was always the first and last person in my thoughts because I could not leave him, without telling him good bye. He was in bed because he had to go to work the next day, he was so tired when his head hit the pillow at night he was out.

I stood by the bed just staring at him and in my thoughts telling him how sorry I was and that he didn't deserve this, he deserved a better wife, a healthier wife. Why didn't he just leave me? It would have made things so much easier for me. He could tell our sons how much I loved them but that sometimes in life things happen to people. He could have just told them, your mother was at her point of desperation and she snapped and things happen in life.

I did not know how long I stood there staring at him; as he turned and saw the blade of a knife, just the blade; thoughts of Vietnam again invaded his territory. Charlie had come back to haunt him in the still of the night. Without thinking he grabbed the knife or at least tried to take the knife away from me and then the struggled began. He was now my enemy and he was taking something away from me. In his mind, I was "Charlie", I was the enemy and he was going to take that knife away from me. In my mind he was the enemy. Thankfully he knew where I was at in my mind and just wanted to get that knife away from me. It might have just been minutes but it seems like forever as we struggled. Finally, he got the knife out of my hand.

We both sat on the bed and cried, what else could we do? He cried and told me he didn't know how to help me anymore and that he loved me but didn't know what to do. He had sent me to the best medical doctors and did whatever he could. I in turn told him I was tired of living the way I was. I was in so much pain. I felt awful because my hair had been cut, my weigh was going up and down; I just hated living.

No person should have to live the way that I did. Why was this happening to me? At time there was nothing else that Tony could do but take me in his arms and rock me like a baby telling me everything was going to be alright and that he would always be there for me no matter what. As always Tony hated going to work. There was nothing he could really do for me. I felt he needed to get away from me to get his mind together.

Tony wanted someone to stay with me. No way! What was he thinking? I would have probably scared who ever stayed with me the first five minutes they spent with me. Now left alone with my train of thoughts somewhere out there, I became desperate again. Desperate again to attempt suicide, I felt desperate because there was nothing else for me; at least that is what I was thinking. When you're in that frame of mind and cannot see the past, the present, or the future, there is nothing, nothing left and Satan, the Devil will creep into a person's mind.

Once again the deceiver of all mankind, was knocking at my door, it is like he is waiting in the wings, waiting there just so he can take you out. In my train of thoughts I didn't know what was happening. Where was God? Had God given up on me? I just didn't know where to turn, who to turn to and I felt lost, not knowing which direction in the roads of life to take.

I had been going to so many doctors at this point in my life. If a Doctor gives you a prescription, unless you tell whatever Doctor you are seeing what medications you are taking I don't think they check to see what prescriptions other Doctors give their patients. I don't blame any of my Doctors for the amount of pills that I was given and because I didn't say anything I had many prescription pills. I would never blame any of my Doctors for giving me as much medications as they did because I feel they were doing it in my best interest.

I had to find pills and it had to be prescription pills because in my mind at the time they were the healers. Taking pills would put me in a state of mind of no comprehension. This particular day I went through my house franticly looking for bottles of prescription pills. One bottle turned to ten, then twenty, thirty, forty, fifty; I ended up with 52 bottles. Pills for pain, pills to get up, pills to go to sleep, pills to help me eat, pills to stop me from eating, and it went on and on. I thought, is this it? I figured I would just start taking these pills, and gorging myself with the pills. I would take them all until I couldn't take anymore. In my weaken state of mind, this was the only way out, of my miserable sick mind.

I remember looking at the bottles, the dates and the Doctors name hoping I could remember why I was given that particular medication, hoping in the back of my mind something would tell me to stop. I would grab a bottle and try to open it. I couldn't open it and I was getting angry with myself, because something as simple as opening the caps was not happening. I was swearing to myself and saying how I was a loser, that I couldn't even open these stupid amber or white bottles. I forgot that I had had surgery on my hand; all this was affecting the opening of the bottles.

Now once again I felt so much a loser. Once again I felt so much a failure that I couldn't even open the caps of those stupid prescription bottles that was there on the floor next to me. I was always repeating things to myself, hoping that if I repeated it enough time, something would make sense to me. I sat in the middle of my living room with these 52 bottles of prescription pills and just hated myself. Hate is such a word of self-destruction. For me I did detest every aspect of my life, whatever life that was.

Sitting in the middle of my living room floor, I thought what is happening to me, to my life. I was still angry at the fact that I couldn't open the prescription bottles, I mean something as insignificant as opening prescription bottles was turning my life at that moment into a hellish nightmare. This was what it was like; I would go on and on about a particular thing, because at the moment it was like I couldn't think of anything else do.

Whenever I needed my medication I would just tell Tony and he always had it ready for me. Okay I said to myself, if I can't get rid of myself one way I'll do it another way. I did not want to live another day in my life if I had to live life the way I was living. Getting up, I went to the bathroom and found my husband's razor and took the blades out and sat down. I kept thinking I can do this, I can't do this, I can do this, I can't do this. It wouldn't be fair to Tony or my sons, to live there life thinking that his wife and their mother had stoop so low, so I went to my bedroom and laid in bed putting the razor under my pillow.

Tony got home from work that night and things were no different, he looked so tired and I despised myself for putting him in this situation. That night we went to bed and I could hear him snoring lightly, thoughts of the day's event and everything was flashing through my head like a video that never stopped, it played on and on and over and over again. I couldn't hear anything but someone was screaming in my head, what a loser.

Like the devil himself who slowly creeps into our lives, it was like he was talking to me, loser! loser! loser! So I took the razor blade that I had hidden under my pillow and in bed I started to slowly slit my wrist, going up and down, as if nothing in the world mattered. Then I hear someone's voice yelling I could hear Tonys voice yelling at me, "What are you doing? Why! "

Taking the razor blade away from me he looked at my wrist. There were 27 cuts and because my hands were so weak I couldn't cut it deep enough, but enough for it to be bleeding. I sat up in the bed and he looked at me crying, and he said you know I am going to have to call the doctor; I have no other choice. I was just staring into space like there was no one around me, my life just sucked. As usual, once again, I ended up in the suicide intensive care unit of a mental hospital.

Before I go on I need to explain something. I really thought long and hard about writing certain things in my book. My thoughts were always how would family members feel, the only person that was my main concern was my mother and how it would affect her. I called my mother one night and told her about the book and what was written in the book. I told her how she would feel about the book and how other family members might feel if this book was written, because the public would be reading about her daughter and about her family.

She said, Noe, "If it helps one person then that's all that matters". I never had any intention in hurting anyone's feelings let alone my families especially Tony's or my sons. Although my mother has passed away, she will always be there with me.

I wondered if I ever decided to publish this book if it would be an embarrassment to anyone because of what was written. How could I leave anything out without telling the true story, the things that were so much a part of my life, the things that I have to live with day in and day out? There was no way I could leave or omit anything.

Whatever the case may be, I would not leave anything out that I thought was important and hope for the best. I remember growing up in Hawaii in the little town of Kaneohe, there was a Hospital that we use to call the mental hospital, the nut house; we were kids then and that's what I knew about it. One of my best friend's Mother worked there. Sometimes I would talk to her about this place where she worked, and now my thoughts were right there.

Continuing with my story I ended up in the suicide intensive care unit of one of the mental hospital. I mean most people don't end up there unless there is a probable cause that that certain individual needs to be there. Normally you hear someone saying that's a 51/50.

This particular time, Tony was to take me just turned out to be so sad. When Tony told me he was taking me somewhere, in my mind it would be a happy place. You see it was close to our wedding anniversary and I thought he was taking me somewhere to celebrate. But it was not a celebration to be, it was the Mental Hospital. Now that I was in the facility it was like an out of body experience, you are there but you are not there, how could I be in this hospital? How could I be in this "lock down" ward? Every door you pass, it shuts, and then you hear the clicking of a lock, then silence.

If you pass someone, who is that person, why are they here? In the facility where I was at, each room had two beds, one desk and your meal was brought to you; because of the high suicide rate the utensils are plastic. When I walked in, because of my state of mind, I was like a robot just following instructions. If you said go I went, if you said stop, I stopped.

That night zoned out; I laid in bed in the hospital room just staring into nowhere and finally fell asleep. For some reason I woke up and turned and there standing next to my bed was this big six foot tall male patient just staring at me; this facility was for male and females. I started yelling at him to get out of my room and telling him I was going to kill him, I told him I didn't care if you were a guy, I will kill you.

I kept screaming. The nurses came running into my room and chased the guy out but by now I was yelling I am going to kill him and I turned around and yelled at the nurses and now I am going to kill you. I was given medication to calm me down and that's the way they did it; pills to wake me up, pills to calm me down, pills to eat, pills to sleep.

Every hospital has their own programs for each patient. During the day there were arts and crafts and different groups you can get into. I would be totally confused when we had group sessions. If I didn't talk they would encourage me to talk and say something. Other times I would talk so much and couldn't shut up they would tell to be quiet or go back to the room. I was in a daze the first time I went there; I didn't know where I was at and I didn't care. If another patient stepped in my space, then whatever way I reacted to them was their problem; of course it would then become the problem of the doctors and nurses that were there, and then if they couldn't handle me it would become Tony's problem.

One day while I was lying in bed I looked across the room and the door was open. As I looked at the bed, I saw Jesus lying in this particular bed, when He sat up he had on a white robe and long hair. He sat up and looked at me and smiled and I smiled back. Later that night while in group session this guy walks in; he was tall and skinny and had long hair. He smiled at me and I thought Jesus is in here to heal the sick and hurting, He has come to rescue me. I remember telling one of the nurses about this guy. She looked at me strange and told me there was no one like that. When I say my psychiatrist and told him I saw Jesus today in your facility, he looked at me like she has really flipped. Till today I know what I saw, I know God had sent an angel to watch over me.

After I got out of the hospital things went back to normal for me. Getting up, taking medication and just lying in bed doing absolutely nothing. That was my life, afraid, just afraid to do anything. I tried to watch TV but nothing interested me. It was like my life had come to a halt. I got up just waiting till I could go back to sleep. I still had a lot of pain but I had been given some different medication that was helping.

When I came home, it seemed things would be fine but then I would find myself going into a depression state of mind. In 1999, I had another carpal tunnel done. Was it starting all over again, had God truly turned away from me?

Of course the year 2000 was another year of pain and suffering for me. One day I got up and I couldn't stop bleeding, because I couldn't get a hold of my doctor, the thought of another time I had bled came back to mind.

Tony called an emergency facility and was told to bring me in right away. It was a horrible night and once again, it brought Tony back with thoughts of Vietnam and all the killing because of all the blood that was coming out of me.

Once things calmed down and my Doctor was contacted, the said the best thing to do was for me to have a radical hysterectomy. I remember after the surgery my Doctor came into my room and said I have good news and bad news. Which one do you want to hear first? Well Mrs. D'Aprile, the bad news is we found a tumor the size of a babys head and the good news is we have removed it. I looked at him surprise. My Doctor must now be on drugs. I guess just that look on my face told him, I don't believe you. He said, I figured you wouldn't believe me so here is the tumor in tack and here is another picture cut in half so that you can see there is no tumor. If I wasn't lying on the bed, I probably would have felled down.

The next surgery was another knee surgery. The year was flying by for me, but thoughts of depression never left my sight. Even in 2001, I would spend the month of January and a week in February in a mental hospital. Once again Tony felt that if I went to Hawaii I might feel better. March when I returned I could not get out of my depression state of mind and by April and May I was back at the mental institution.

I don't want people to think that I was crazy, but I was just so depress at the way things were going on in my life. I could never see the rainbow at the end of the day. People are not crazy, just nowhere to turn. I mean it was like my life was constantly repeating itself, Because of my situation and for my safety, I lived in the hospital. There was psychiatric treatment, group therapy, individual therapy. For about 10 hours a day, 7 days a week I was programmed to do what others told me to do. It would take Tony, depending on the traffic anywhere from1 to 2 hours to come to visit me. But every day that I was there, he came. On weekends he spent more time with me. It was really getting hard for him to keep what was going on a secret to my family.

There were times I would just stay in the room, I remember he came to visit me one day and brought my favorite flower, carnations and they were also one of my favorite colors orange. As soon as I got it I threw it on the floor. I hated everything around me.

Now it seemed the only friends I had was my pen and paper because I could write down my feelings on it and no one would see it but me. I would write poem to sort my feelings out. I wrote about the good things that I had in my life and the things that overshadowed my life. At times I would plead with God to help me fight this sickness that I had and then at times I would talk to the devil as if he was my friend. My mind would play games with me, and I was constantly trying to find my way out of this fog. The outside world meant absolutely nothing to me because for me I lived in just my world and in this time of my life I didn't want anyone in my world.

I would go through bouts of depression or wanting to commit suicide a thousand times, but just kept it to myself. I was told I had a chemical in-balance in my brains and was told I was a bi-polar manic depression person. When I was down, there was no bottom and when I was high there was no top.

For me the mental hospitals saved my life, it was there that I was with other patients who were going through the same problems as I was, but each was at a different level. The many times that I spent in these hospitals helped me understand the human brain. You can use it to your advantage or let it destroy you. I still go through bouts of depression and sometimes it scares me because I don't want to get so depressed that I end up where I did.

Taking pills will always be an issue with me, and maybe there will come a day that I won't have to take any but I realize that is not going to happen. I realize that God allows things to happen for a purpose, we may not understand it at the time but He reveals it to us later. I also realize that the Devil is right there ready to step in if we allow him to. Following are more poems I wrote during that period in time. As you read the poems you will see where my mind set was at that particular time. I'm sure many people write poetry or short notes to themselves and would be ashamed if anyone read it, but I came to the conclusion, it does not matter anymore. You come to the point in life where you say this is me. Take me or leave as I am. You can see where my mind and feelings took me by the following pomes I wrote.

It's My Time to Die

Look at the sky crying for me, look at the raindrop but it's only a teardrop that I see. What did I do wrong again I tried my best, and all it ever gets me is into one big mess. There is no beauty when I look around, the four corners of the building it is so cold in town, I'm getting silent but the fire in me is still burning, so I have to sit and do some journaling.

Should I have done this or should I have done that, it doesn't matter I don't care where I'm at. It's my time to die, it is my time to say goodbye, it's a shame I wanted to give, but I'm running out of options to live. I guess I'll be quiet and stick to myself, and then maybe I won't hurt anyone else. Why do I have to be sorry all the time, I guess dying is better than losing my mind. It's my time please God call me, you brought me here now set me free.

There is no beauty in life everything's cold, like when you go to the graveyard all those dead souls. Will I ever be happy or live in despair? I don't know I don't really care. I'm so unhappy if I could only hide, because all I want to do is die inside. It's my turn to die the time is ticking fast, my straw has been pulled, freedom at last, to those who remember me when I am out of this world, just remember me as a happy little girl. I am innocent can't they see, then why do I feel like everyone is picking on me. I'll be alone even if everyone cares to show affection now I don't dare. Don't hug me, don't touch me, for I am no good, it's my time to die, I'm in that kind of mood.

A Note to God

Please carry my burden do not despair for God has shifted the storm elsewhere. Right now it seems all else has failed, but He's sending something through the heavenly mail. I again want to have a passion for life, one where I don't have to use a gun or a knife. I want to see the birds fly like an airplane that flies through the sky.

If there is supposed to be success in all that I do, give me wisdom, courage, and determination too. Let me challenge with an understanding heart, and when I leave, with love I will depart.

Suicide

Suicide, remember me? I am the one who will set you free, I am the one who told you, you were the best, and I am the one who told you, you didn't need the rest. The circumstances in your life were under my control, I was the one who told you not to let go. I demanded so much from you, now everything you didn't want to happen is coming true.

Broken Heart

I'm so sad I don't know why all I ever do is cry. My heart is broken the cut is deep; I don't think I will be able to sleep.

Regrets I have known, I've accomplished a lot and if I don't make it then it doesn't matter if I flop. If you walked a mile in my shoes if only for a day, you would get down on your knees and beg God to take you away.

I live a fine line between good and bad, never knowing to be happy or sad. Don't look at my face do you think you know who I am, God gave me a gift but I still don't understand.

See Thru My Eyes

I sit in silence looking around, wondering what I am doing in this part of town. I wish I could tell you how I feel I wish I could tell you if only I knew.

If you see thru my eyes, you'd wish you weren't here, because all you will feel is sadness and fear. Its loneliness and sorrow if you see thru my eyes sit and talk to me before you say goodbye.

What happen to my friends they left long ago, when things got hectic and my life hit low? See thru my eyes and a tear you will see, I wish you could cry and cry with me.

CHAPTER SEVEN
Drugs! Drugs!! And more Drugs!!!

"He heals the brokenhearted and binds up their wounds"
Psalm 147:3

It was a beautiful day and the sun was out. I could hear the sound of birds chirping, but as beautiful as the day was, I felt like I was drowning. It seemed like I would come up for air only to be knocked down again and again. I sat in the room of this mental hospital, here I am again I said to myself, won't it ever end? Later, I went out to watch the other patients play volleyball. Growing up in Hawaii, volleyball was my favorite game and like most sport you had to move a lot. The only thing I hated about the game was when someone on the other team decides to slam the ball.

As I sat there and watched the other patients play volleyball, I reflected back at a time almost 16 years ago when I last played volleyball. At that time I bent down to hit the ball and went to low and slammed my knees into the cement. I got up and got out of the game and sat as I watched everyone play. That night I went to bed with my knees so sore. Getting up the next morning I couldn't move my knees and it was hurting worse, when I looked at my knee it was twice its size. I made an appointment to see my doctor and was told I would have to have knee surgery.

The knee surgery was called an Arthroscopic knee surgery. This procedure is among the most common orthopedic surgical procedures. They go in using a small camera and it allows an orthopedic surgeon to diagnose and treat any knee disorder because they have a clear view of the inside of the knee. Like any surgery whether big or small you still have pain, and yes you are still prescribed medication to help you endure the pain.

Taking prescription was rare for me at the time. I had always stayed pretty healthy. When my boys were born I had to have them by caesarean section. In this type of surgery incisions are made through a mother's abdomen to deliver the baby. The reason I give a little information of certain surgeries is so that a person has a better understanding of my story. At that time there was a little concern health wise, but now days it is a common procedure. When you have back problems like I was having that don't help either.

Even though I have tried to put the years in chronological order, as you can see I will also take you out of order. My life had now taken a different direction; my road to health and happiness had turned 365 degrees. In my life what had been a healthy me with no prescriptions prescribed to me, now it seemed everywhere I turned, you could find a bottle somewhere in my house.

I was going to different doctors as I had stated earlier and no one was keeping track of which doctor I was going to and the amount of prescriptions I was taking. I had to take so many in a day, so by the end of 1997 I was taking almost 40 pills a day, not all different ones maybe about 10 different pills. Also, there were the shots of Demerol, versed, and vistaril for pain; pills of morphine, percadin and tegretol. I was having problems with my skin which caused me to itch all the time. Many times I would scratch till I bled and wanted to dig my skin out because the itching wouldn't stop. I took prednisone, vancenase for allergies and inflammation, and Zantacs to prevent ulcers. Then I was given different creams to help me, elocon, carmol, eurax, lotrimin, lotrisone, xylocaine and bactroban.

For drugs, 1998 would turn into my worst nightmare. Three surgeries and then more medication was pump into me so that I felt like a zombie. I was prescribed Tylenol with codeine #4, xanax, ametidine, atarax carafate, ceftin, cimetidie, clonidine, diflucna, etodolac, lidocaine, lodine, oxycodone, ranitidie, etc. Because of the attempts at suicide, I was given drugs for anxiety, panic attacks, and insomnia. Then there was ativan, buspar, chloral hydrate, klonopin, dalmane, paxil, restoril, temazepan to name a few.

Those days I would just lie in bed and stare at the ceiling, alive but not alive. My eyes were open but I could not see. When someone spoke to me they might as well have talked to someone on the moon. I would look at you, but I saw absolutely nothing. I always had this wide eye gaze and I didn't know if a person was in front of me or not.

The year 1999 ended with more pills of elivil, neurontin, prempro, ultram and going in for epidural shots. The year 2000 more drugs were added such as lamical, lorcet, topamax, singuliar, cetrizine, dovonex, tetracycline, doxcycline, phenegram. If we didn't have health insurance we would have been flat broke with nothing. Tony with his common sense always made sure we had some kind of insurance. In fact, one insurance agent told us we had too much. Tony felt a person can never have too much insurance.

My communication with people started to dwindle. I didn't want to be with anyone other than Tony or my sons. I hated looking into the mirror because what looked back at me was not someone I knew. I was tired of repeating things to different people; I didn't want to be looked at as a druggy. When the phone rang, my only thoughts were, who is calling me now and what am I going to say.

When I would talk to anyone, I would find myself rambling on and on about nothing, absolutely nothing. The person listening to me didn't know how to tell me you're repeating yourself. I wanted to isolate myself from the whole world. Crying spells came and went; depression all the time.

My days were now spent on keeping track of the many medications that I was taking; my self-esteem took a nose dive. Because of the medication and lack of exercise due to health reasons; I began to gain weigh then lose it, then gain it back and lose it. It was like going up and down on a roller coaster. A new problem arose; now due to the many medications taken my hair was starting to fall out.

At that time I looked back on the first 50 years of my life. Times had changed and this painting that I had started bits and pieces of my life coming together but the painting still not completed.

I still was confused by so many turn of events. For now, God had continued to be my guide and I knew He would see me through whatever trials and tribulations that came my way even if I couldn't see it. The painting of my life's picture was not complete but now it had a wide variety of rainbow colors.

For me at times I felt like I was drowning in water and not being able to save myself. My mother's prayers had always been answered as I remember her so many times praying for God to take care of all her children wherever they were.

Then somewhere through all this fog, through the lost wilderness, through all the pills and medications, somewhere I began to see the rainbow. My palette of different colors was starting to come back.

CHAPTER EIGHT
WITH A SONG IN MY HEART

"I will praise You, O Lord, among the peoples,
And I will sing praises to you among the nations."
Psalms 108:3

From the time I was a young girl in Hawaii, music has always been a part of my life. As a child in Hawaii I grew up in what I called a semi musical family. At family gatherings my Uncle David would play his saxophone and my Aunty Katie her accordion. There were times my cousin Lokelani would play the piano. My cousin Pasty had a beautiful high soprano voice and she sang a lot of Hawaiian songs. My sister Omi also has a beautiful soprano voice and I loved harmonizing with her. My brother Wayne and cousin Louie and Blossom also loved to sing; other family members would join in, as the years passed by soon the nieces and nephews joined in.

I also loved to sing and when my family got together if there was a piano I would grab a chair sit down and play the piano. The family would gather together and from where ever they were sitting would join in the singing. I also loved to play the ukulele; once in a great while I would play the organ. After I had the surgery under my arm when they took the tumor our and it damaged the nerves, things changed for me. I couldn't play the piano or strum the ukulele that well without feeling a lot of pain in my fingers, eventually I would give my oldest grandson Nikko my piano and once in a while I would play the ukulele. But God had not let me down, when I would cry cause I couldn't play the piano, I could hear his voice saying, you must make a joyful sound unto the Lord.

My love for the piano started years ago in Hawaii. When the family got together my cousin Lokelani, would sit at the piano and play the piano and sing at the same time. I would watch her as her fingers went up and down at the keyboard, and told myself I wanted to be like her and play the piano as she did. You could say it was her that really influenced my love for music and playing the piano. Sad to say she died at an early age but till today I think of her and miss her beautiful smile and her awesome voice.

During the sixth or seventh grade I wanted to take piano lessons. I knew financially for my mom to pay for the lessons it would not be possible. My mom asked me how bad do you want to play the piano and would I practice. I promised her if I was able to take piano lessons she would not have to remind me of practicing. I would practice and practice and listen to whatever my piano teacher said. My mother agreed and got in touch with the piano teacher and it was a go. Till the day my mother died she never regretted paying for those piano lessons.

I didn't have a piano to practice on at home but I was able to practice the piano in school. One day I came home from school, low and behold there was an old upright piano in the living room. I was so excited I sat to play even though the piano was not tuned, and some of the keys were missing plus the pedals on the bottom didn't work. To me it was as if I had received a new piano. When I think back about those days I can just imagine what it sounded like, but to me and my mom it was music to our ears.

Days turned into week and I continued practicing and going to my piano classes. On one particular day I came home and there was no piano in the house, it had finally happen. I found out that my playing was so bad because of the out of tune piano and the keys missing, that the piano had been moved into a shack that was on the property. There were so all kinds of junks in the shack and I had to climb over them to get to the piano and it still was practice, practice, practice.

My piano teacher had said, no matter how flat the piano is, just be sure my fingering was right. I use to run the scales up and down. I practiced sonatas, waltzes, and any type of classical music. Whenever I had the extra money I would buy me music sheets or books; this was in the early 60's and music then was cheap. You could buy a sheet of music for 75 cents, now they run anywhere from $3.00 to $5.00 a song. Babysitting was another way to get extra money, so I was always looking for babysitting jobs. Times were really getting hard for my mom and the money was just not there. After about 9 months I had to stop taking lessons. When I told my piano teacher I had to quit and why, she said it didn't matter because I had done so well in my classes. I would continue my studies even if it was on my own.

To continue my own study in music, I began to play the piano for church and started singing in the church as well as school choir. Sometimes my choir teacher would ask me to

play the piano. I loved music and there was always a song in
my heart. Most of the music I played was sacred or classical
music. I wanted to expand and learn other types of music
and I would spend 3 or 4 hours a day just practicing. After
I got out of high school, I went to California and spent one
year in college. I majored in music. As exciting as it was,
I would have my biggest disappointment there. I was now
taking piano lessons at the college level, while there my
music professor calls me into his office to talk to me and to
see what my goals were. I told him that my biggest dream
at the time was to play in Carnegie Hall. He looked me
straight in the face and said, "You will never play there".

Here I was at a Seventh Day Adventist collage and instead
of giving me some kind of encouragement especially since it
was my first year in college, I get this disappointing news.
At that time I was a shy island girl and thought you know
he must be right. I never questioned him. I was working
my way through college and wasn't going to waste my
money if I wasn't going to attain my goal. Without talking
to anyone, I decided college was not for me. Discouraged
and disappointed after the school year was up I never went
back. Regrets because of that, not really, maybe my life
would have been different; but then I would not have been
writing this book.

After that year I began to do my own practicing and
learning about music in my own way. At this point in time
I had continued being in contact with Tony.

Although we were far away from each other we continued
writing to each other or calling each other on the telephone.
After Tony got out of the Marine Corps he moved to
California. By now I had decided to drop out of college

and concentrated more on what life had to offer me other than college. I had found an apartment for Tony; he had been sending me money so that I could pay the rent and buy things for the apartment. It was nice because it was just about 5 minutes from my sisters' house.

Tony was out of the Marine Corps, but he was still in the reserves, and I knew they could call him back if it was necessary anytime, but for now we were just young lovers and we wanted to spend the rest of our lives together. June 29, 1969, Tony and I were married in Riverside, California.

Now life took a different turn for me. Happily married and finally on my own, I would tell my husband Tony about the college situation and how much I had wanted to play the piano in Carnegie Hall. Now I had other hopes and dreams but I had wanted to continue playing the piano. Tony bought me a piano and I would spend hours and hours playing the piano.

During this time I met up with a Polynesian entertainment group, and would get involved with performing with them. I would become the lead singer in their group and we did different luau shows. I also did singing telegrams; where someone would call and want a singer to sing to a specific person for their birthday, anniversary or any other occasion.

At this point in time I had a big decision to make. The leader of the group wanted me to go full time in the entertainment business. I had talked to Tony about the situation and he said, you have to decide for yourself. I had to really think about how our lives would change, there would be practicing and then going all over the place to entertain. The money was good and I met a lot of people but I was also so much in love with Tony. I knew that the time I spent on practicing and then doing different Hawaiian shows would take so much of my time and energy away from my marriage. Had I been single it would have been different. I figured my marriage was more important and the entertainment business would take up to much of my time. The leader of the group was disappointed but she understood. During the years to follow she would call me up to do a gig or two. I eventually stopped doing any outside entertainment altogether.

Now not singing for money did not stop me from singing altogether. There were so many avenues that I could take and use my musical talent elsewhere. I played the piano and sang for church. There were weddings, and funerals and parties and so many other things I could do with my musical talent.

One day Tony decided to look into finding some military organization that he could get involve with. Tony was Marine Corps all the way, 24/7. I had learned to accept his ways and ideals about the Marine Corps. He was also a Vietnam Veteran and had wanted to see if he could find other Vietnam Veterans. It was around 1972 and he was still in the Marine Corps reserves. He located an organization called the VFW; Veterans of Foreign War, and became a member of Post 9223. He wasn't too much involved with the organization but went to some of their functions. It wouldn't be till over 20 years later that I decided to get involved with the Ladies Auxiliary of the Veterans of Foreign War, Post 9223.

Walking into the club one day with Tony, I met two ladies; Jenny whose husband had been one of the commanders there (but her husband was now deceased) and Donnie who was the bartender at the time. Jenny and Donnie were both members of the Ladies Auxiliary of the VFW there. They wanted me to join the Ladies Auxiliary and I really liked both of them and felt that here was a chance for me to get involved with something that my husband was involved in. Through the years I've come to know both of them, "their friendship to me is priceless". Jenny was also from Hawaii, so that made our friendship extra special. I always looked forward to seeing Jenny and Donnie at the VFW, Post 9223. Jenny was the cook at the club and our conversations always ended up with talking about Hawaii and our love for the little island in the Pacific.

I decided to join the Ladies Auxiliary of the VFW there and till today have never regretted it. I didn't know if I wanted to get involved in the organization or just be a member that joined. Of course as the years have gone by I have taken many offices there, and have been involved in the different functions that they have.

One day, one of the Veterans, a United States Marine asked if Tony and I would like to go with him to one of the Veteran hospital located in Loma Linda, California. It actually is a Medical Facility but most people just call it the VA hospital. This Marines name was Walt, and he explained that they had a nursing home within the facility. Many of our wounded and sick veterans stayed and of course many also died there. I wasn't too sure if I wanted to go, I didn't know what to expect.

Walt said, come out on the nights when they had bingo and see what it was all about, so Tony and I did. We started going on bingo nights and there I would meet the men and once in a while ladies that had put their live on the line, so that we may live in the land of the free. There were other veterans from our VFW that also came to volunteer. During Bingo we would serve juice and popcorn, and after the bingo games we served deserts. It was then that I really realized, freedom isn't free and the cost of war was paid by these veterans and all our veterans. It was here that I would start to understand about PTSD; Post Traumatic Stress Disorder and other veteran issues.

Usually after bingo when desserts were served, you could hear different veterans talking or at times it got quiet. From day one I had noticed a piano in the room that we had bingo in, and I thought, wouldn't it be nice if I could play some music while they were eating and put some music in their lives at least for the moment. I talked to Walt and mention about playing the piano and he thought it was a good idea. On some bingo nights usually after bingo I would play the piano and theses veterans really enjoyed it. There were other times I would bring my karaoke machine and sing to these Veterans.

Walt was in charge of bingo when we were there, he always have had a passion to help any and all veterans and their family members. Walt became and still is very good friends with Tony and I. I looked forward every time I went to bingo to see the veterans that I had met, knowing that in some ways I was bringing some kind of joy into their lives.

At times some of the Veterans would give me things. There was this Veteran named Tony who was blind, one bingo night while talking to him he told me he had something to give me. He handed me a box and in the box he had painted a set of horse head bookends. I was amazed because of the fact that he was blind. Another patient Phil; he was tall and lanky and had problems seeing, he had a hard time with his eye lids and was always having to open his eye lids with his fingers. One day he said Francine I made you something, he had painted this item and it was so cute but here again I was amazed because of the problems that he had seeing and just so thankful that these veterans thought enough of me to make me something even in their situation.

One night in came this guy on a wheel chair, he really looked young and his head was all bandaged up. He was loud when he talked and some of the patients around him seem agitated with him there. I went up to him told him my name and started to talk and listen to him, I found out he was a Marine and he seem to be mad with the world, mad with the situation he was in angry at life and now what seemed no life at all. Boy could I relate to him.

Now let me depart from this part of my story. After I had brain surgery I was embarrassed because my hair had been cut. I didn't want anyone seeing that ball spot plus because of the type of surgery I had, the surgeon had never put a plate to cover the hole where the surgery was done, so from that day till even now, I still feel at times like I have a big hole in the left side of the back of my head and I still have problems.

One day my husband bought me a baseball cap, but on the top it said "USMC" which stood for United States Marine Corps. This way I could have my head covered and not be embarrassed and I was also flying his colors so to speak "The United States Marine Corps".

Well when we went to the different military base or was at any military function that sold caps, that had anything relating to the United States Marine Corps or Vietnam Veterans we bought it. Tony would buy these caps so that I always had different ones to use. I got so use to wearing them that I didn't feel right if I didn't have it on.

Now getting back to this young Marine, as he talked to me you could see the pain in his face. I listened to him and told him I understood how he felt and I knew how he must be hurting and I also understood about his brain injury. I don't know what it was with this Marine, if he was so angry that he felt no one understood him or that here was a volunteer telling him she understood him. He looks straight at me, whips his cap off and say, look I just have half a head, because I got messed up in the war! What do you know about hurting and pain? Well some of the other patients around him knew me and was just sitting there seeing what was going to happen next.

Whether fate had brought me together with this patient, or God had put him there for a reason for us to meet; I always remember what my husband said, in the Marine Corps you adapt and improvise to the situation you're in. In my head I kept thinking, you're such a jerk, I just told you I was a Marine's wife and you think you're going to scare me. Oh you may be big and angry at the world but I didn't put you in that situation. No one told you to sign up for the Corps. Of course I wasn't angry at him and some of the other patients were telling him to shut up, I told them to stand down.

I looked this Marine in the eye and told him, I am sorry you feel the way you do and the situation you are in. As far as your pain, I and no one else knows how you feel and what you are going through. I have been through my own hell and been through my own pain so let me tell you my story. I told him some of my medical history and he was quiet the whole time. Then he said, I guess you do understand the pain and hurt that I am going through, after that he did quiet down.

Every time I went to the nursing home, there was this patient; his name was Lucky. He really didn't talk to anyone and always seem to be in so much pain also. One night I got to the nursing home early and I started up a conversation with him. He told me that when he was in Vietnam he was a sniper. He didn't like doing what he was doing but that was his job. I know a lot of people don't like snipers and I can understand why. Basically their job is to kill a certain individual. The more I listen to Lucky tell me of the things that he had to do, I realize "kill one, save many".

Lucky would tell me about his pain and suffering and I said, where do you hurt Lucky, and then he said I wish I could tell you, but I hurt all over. You could look and see agony written all over his face, in other words it was his whole body. He said, you know I listen to you play the piano; do you sing? I said, I like sing but that doesn't mean I can sing. He said I use to like this song called "The Old Rugged Cross", do you know it? I said yes and he said will you sing it for me. I said okay and went over the piano and sang the song for him. When it was done he gave me a smile and thanked me. I gave him a hug and I could feel his body trembling, I could feel his bones like he had nothing left on his body. That thank you and smile, made it worthwhile going to bingo that night.

The next time I came in I couldn't wait to see Lucky and talk to him.   He wasn't at bingo that night. I asked one of the guys if they had seen Lucky, they told me that he had passed away. The sadness I felt that night would be one that would make me have a different attitude. I went home that night and in the still of the night I told God, Lucky is out of his pain and misery. Lucky reminded me of the thief on the cross. When Jesus was crucified and nailed to the cross He suffered the most horrible, disgraceful punishment known. It was considered so horrible that it was used only for slaves.

In the bible, the New King James Version in Luke 23:32-43, it talks about "The King on a Cross". The soldiers are mocking Jesus and telling him if He is the King then save Himself. There were two criminals, one on the left and one on the right with Him. One of the criminals who was to be hanged blasphemed Jesus by saying "If you are the Christ then save yourself and us." The other one a thief said, "Do you not even fear God, and says that God has done nothing wrong. The thief turns and says to Jesus, "Lord, remember me, when you come into your kingdom."

I thought about Lucky, how he had gone to Vietnam and was a sniper. As a sniper he took lives and now here he was back in the United States telling me how he regretted doing what he had to do but it was his job. It was like telling me his story, how he had taken so many lives. How he had disrupted these individuals' families and now he was safe in the USA. The killings must have haunted him, and like the thief who was so ashamed for what he did, so was Lucky. For Lucky to tell me his stories it was like he was saying please understand, it was my job. I told Lucky, when you are in the Marine Corps or any other job, you follow instructions and that is what you did. But like the thief on the cross, I think that night Lucky was talking to me, God understood him and had placed me there to talk to me, and sometimes I wonder, was Lucky an angel who was talking to me letting me know that somewhere down the road things would change in my life.

I truly believe God allowed me to go through all my suffering so that I could understand those I would come in contact with later in my life. I could go on and on and tell stories of different veterans that I met and how their lives had changed since the war, but it would have to be in another book all by itself.

One day I was talking to Walt at the VFW and we were looking at the piano up stage, no one ever played it. I told Walt, do you think they would let me play the piano? He said he would talk to someone about it. About a month later Walt said that if I wanted to I could play the piano while people were eating dinner. So I started playing dinner music for those who dined there. I truly believe God will put certain individuals in our lives and we don't know why until God reveals it to us. I thank God that Walt became a part of Tony and my life. Not only is Walt a Marine, and a very proud Marine, but he has a good heart and understand people so well. Every time I turn around he is always trying to help someone. We still have continued to be good friends but we all lead our own lives. Walt when you read this book, I want to thank you for your kindness towards me and my family, for all the time you had to listen to me talk and talk and talk.

All my life I felt God had a purpose in my life, especially with music. Music just makes me feel good. At the VA facility where we went to, I went around to the different patients there and asked them what some of their favorite songs were or what kind of songs they liked. After I made a list of the songs, I found the background music and then I sat down and recorded me singing the songs on a cassette. I knew it would be expensive to buy a bunch of cassettes and then trying to record them, well God does things in mysterious ways. I told Tony what I wanted to do. One day he came home and gave me all these brand new blank cassettes. I told him where did you get it from, he said he was telling people at work what I wanted to do and when he came home that night someone had put 100 blank cassettes in our truck. We never knew where it came from, but the joy I saw on these Veterans faces when I gave it to them was worth it all. Was there a guardian angel that had dropped it there?

When I was in one of the mental hospitals, there was a room where you could go in and visit with family and friends. In this room they also had a piano. After visitation was over there was nothing to do and people would just sit around just staring into space. I would get up and play the piano; every once in a while I would also sing. Soon patients were coming in just to hear me play the piano and sing. At times they would give me a request and then join me in singing if they knew the words. Each individual would listen; each in their own thoughts, in their own little world. This would also take our minds away from any negativity we had. For me it would always bring me back to when I was growing up in Hawaii and thinking of the church I had been raised in.

Music is so much a part of my life. Every song that I sing takes me down memory lane to a place that brought me a lot of happiness. If I wasn't singing while playing the piano, then I would strum my ukulele and sing. When I got sick the music stopped. Because of the tumor that was removed on the right side of my arm and the two carpal tunnels I had which was also on the right hand; I couldn't play the piano or ukulele for a long time. Because of mental problems, I just had a time trying to remember songs that I had knew so well.

Now days I rarely play the piano or ukulele mainly because of the problems I do have with my hand. When I have a chance I go to Karaoke and there I get to sing the songs that I like to sing. The colors of the rainbow are starting to come back now, although very slow. I am very careful as to what I say and to whom I say it.

Maybe the palette of paint that I had thought had all dried up are going to start coming back. Maybe there is still hope, and inspiration that I can bring to others, that I sometimes find it hard to find in my life. The only hope I have is that every day I open my eyes, and hear the birds sing, I know there is a God and He is watching over me and seeing the direction that I am taking.

CHAPTER NINE
LET THE HEALING BEGIN

Because of what has happen to me in the last 9 or 10 years, I didn't want to look to the future. Looking to the future for me was like looking at a rainbow, I saw so many different colors like the colors of life but never seen the end, because the color of my rainbow always seemed to be gray; uncertainty.

After what had taken place, years would pass by before I went back to what I call my one on one with God. Thinking about what had happen and what has happen since then I now know that God had always been on my side from the very beginning. Within my very soul I now know he never left or deserted me. He has been there before I was born, when he gave me life to enter this world and will be there everlasting. We live in a world of uncertainty and you tell me something, something that I cannot see is out there, do I really believe you? I have faith in God, but is He really out there?

Now over 60 years old, I look at things the way I did when I lived in Hawaii. To me life has to be simple. If a person does not have that one on one with God, if you cannot include Him in your daily living then something for me is wrong. I, want my sons to say I got the best Mom, I want my daughter in law to say, I am so glad I married your son, I want my grandchildren to say I have the best Grandmother. If they say that, I can turn around and say, I had the "Best", through me you see my Mom and through her, the end results she loved the Lord and I hope in some way, you can see God through me.

What is in the future for me, I really don't know. Sometimes we as humans plan and plan for things we want to happen in the future, we work so that we can save our money for things, bigger homes, better cars and it goes on and on and then these plans just get destroyed. At the end of the day you are left with nothing. We blame everyone else but ourselves. I, on the other hand, totally blamed myself, wondering what I had done wrong, and what I was going to do about it. Had I not been so ill those many years would things have been different? Had God not given me so many talents would things have been different?

All my life I have tried to live up to the way my mother raised me; to be good, kind, caring and most of all turning to God in times of trouble and in time of goodness. When life was the darkest for me I asked God, "If you love me save me". I believe God allowed me to struggle and to continuously see Satan as he is, because only then could I tell my story.

Satan took me to the depths of depression and he kept coming to me in so many ways. When a person does not understand what is happening to them, their life can be turned upside down and in turn everything around them will be upside down, the world will be negative. No matter where the person turns there is no light at the end of the tunnel, the water becomes a drowning pool, everyone that is trying to help you and care for you now there is no trust. Good becomes evil and evil becomes your friend.

What was white is now black, and you are stuck in this black box not being able to get out. No scissors or knife can cut this black box, no hammer can pound this box down no hole is deep enough for you to bury it. It comes to the point where you are so scared you will do anything to get you out of that misery and then Satan the Devil is there waiting. He has that smile that you want to see, he has that voice that is sweet and soft, he has the power to give you riches beyond your belief and all you have to do is follow him. Just one step he says if you can't take that step then you can crawl to me and Satan leads you to where he wants you.

On the other hand you look at God but there you see a struggle, something does not make sense, everything about Satan looks good, you see he has what you want. On Gods corner you see the struggles, you read about His life here on earth and the torture He went to, the cross of the world He had to carry and then the suffering. But there is that voice that says "come to me all that labor and I will give you rest". Lord, why should I follow you when I have to struggle and struggle and carry that cross, when Satan tells me I don't have to do that?

All my life I seem to be going back and forth between good and evil. I use to always turn to my Mom and tell her, well what would you do Ma? Always that smile, always that gentle voice. You need to pray about it, I would go to Tony and tell him, well Honey what would you do? And it was always that smile always that voice of confidence, think about it, pray about it, then think about it again and then pray about it.

I really wanted something to always bring me back to that moment in time when I realize that God was truly my healer. For me singing and the songs I sing are really important, I just don't sing just to sing, it has to mean something to the group of people that I am singing to. I knew that giving a testimony in any Seventh Day Adventist church and then singing would be holding me out to what people would say and feel about me. That is the way I was feeling at the time.

How would God give me healing not only to my hand but to my unforgiving heart, the heart that had turned cold to the church, this church that had been a part of my life since the day I was born?

I always have felt there are testimonies in the songs people sing, and I remember when I was trying to find a song to sing, I kept looking and looking and I told God, it has to be the right song and lo and behold this song appears to me. How I found it I don't know. I changed a lot of the wording in it so that it could fit with my testimony but the story is there, and if I was to only sing the song the words to the song could stand on its own and minister to you.

It is amazing how God will truly give you the knowledge and understanding of anything that you don't understand if He truly believes you are sincere about it. As I look back to that time fame, I think of all the medication that I was taking all the prescription that was given to me it was giving me a chemical imbalance. This caused so much emotional distress and disturbances.

Thank God I'm able to look back to the past and understand that what happened to me; there was a reason for that. The brain surgery and everything that has happen to me continues to leave me physical and mentally uncertain as to how I feel. I realize as a human being I am not perfect and I never will be. I know that I must always look to the cross and remember the struggles of Jesus, the cross that He carried and continues to carry for all of us. Our struggles are nothing compared to what Jesus had to go through, he had to carry the weight of the world.

The word Heal means to make sound or whole, to restore to health. There are many ways a person can be healed, and with all the Doctors I went to and with all the medications that were given me, I still needed more, more of anything, more of everything. I needed something that would make me see how God truly is the Healer of all. God in His loving ways demonstrated to me why He is who He is and blessed me when in His creation He made the perfect mate to help with my healing.

I don't have to thank Tony for giving up so much because he and I are one with each other and I would do the same for him. Part of my healing now is telling my husband how I truly feel. Sometimes we get so busy with our lives we forget to tell the person that has pulled us through, thank you.

My Dear Husband Tony, you have seen hell twice. When you left New York as a young boy and then joined the United States Marine Corps, you saw "hell" as a Vietnam combat Marine. You had to put that hell back in your mind when you came back State side because it is something only you can understand. For all the years I have been with you there are still things in your mind that only you at that time could see and hear. The other hell you saw was with me. You did not ask for the situation that stopped at your doorstep but when it came you saw me during my hell on earth.

Your love and devotion to me lets me know that I am only second to God in your life. You have shown me what it is that makes every obstacle in my life worth fighting for. Both our sons had to struggle to be born into this world. You have always said I am the perfect wife and a good mother and I thank you because you give me the privilege to raise our sons Wayne and Frank.

You have always been a concern and loving father who has kept your relationship with our sons on equal footing. You have been opened minded with them and have always been there when you were needed. I am overwhelmed by your continuous devotion to our sons, giving options to so many things and expressing your opinions even when they fought hard to disagree with you and try to change your mind.

Our grandchildren, Nikko, Nathan, Nalani, Nelissa and our great grandson Caleb would not be here if it was not for you and in my struggles in life they are so much a part of the healing process that I am going through. They are our future and they will carry our legacy.

As a grandfather and great grandfather, your grandkids find you irresistible because you listen to them and talk to them on a level they can understand. There is no I or me in your conversations with them but it is always "them". There is no side stepping when you feel they need to be told the truth on things. Your eagle eyes are always with them wherever they go and although physically you are not there they know it. Sometimes they are disappointed because you are not in agreement with them but they know it is a disagreement with love. As a father in-law, you know our daughter in-law Michelle thinks the world of you, she has gone through many storms with me and I couldn't thank her enough.

Tony, I love you because you have put so much time, energy and patience in our relationships. You showed me how to make this world a better place to live and to strive to reach for my goals no matter what the struggle. The combination of your intellect amazes me.

God allowed us to weather many storms in our lives together. Healing comes in many forms and He has put you in my life so that you are my "healer". When I stumbled you have picked me up. When I needed guidance you have had the answer for me. When I am sad you make me happy, when I cry you make me laugh, when I am angry you calm the storm, when I am confused you take me out of confusion. This is all part of Gods work in healing my soul.

As we travel the road together there will be other struggles in life but I know that God was kind enough to give me a healing hand through you. I now can wake up in the morning and see the sun shine or the rain fall. I can hear my sons and grandchildren calling me. God has granted me healing through you and I am so bless. Someday we will both sit at Jesus' feet, I on the left and you on the right and we will sing a joyful song unto the Lord. I love you.

I was so blessed when God brought Tony into my life.

Our "Special Angel", my grand-daughter Nalani, still by her Grandmothers side, being there when I need her no matter what.

And so my story has come to an end, but the truth is, it is only the beginning. I have lived a good life even with all my health issues because God has always been there for me. I have come full circle, from the church that I left and never wanted to return to, but God has shown me why it is time for me to come home.

I am proud to say I am a Seventh Day Adventist, yes there are things I wish I had never done and even said, but it is all put behind me. My God has called upon me once again, every day I wake up and every night I go to bed I know he is there. He said I will lead you, and I said I will follow. I know that every move I make He is my decision Maker. The world can look at me and say what they want but it doesn't matter.

God has put a new song in my heart. Every step I make is a slow decision but a thought out decision. I know Satan will always be there to tempt me, to put things in front of me and want me to walk with him. But God is my Lily of the valley, He is my Rose of Sharon, He is the fairest of ten thousand. He let me see a world that is dying, because of the Master of Deceit.

He knows that I will always struggle with my health issues because that is the way life is. When my struggle is the greatest I can look to Him and see the struggle that He went through and know that mine is nothing. When I look to the Hill of Calvary, I know the weight of the world and the weight of my struggles He has carried.

Like a child He will lead me, I will be His lamb. He has put forth things in my way and people that will help and guide me. When I decided to take that step forward to get back into the church, I really prayed to God to let me look at Him and not at people in the church. I didn't want to be disenchanted. On one of the days I did go to church there was a signup sheet to meet in small groups in peoples home to study Gods word. We sign up but in my heart I was hoping no one would call.

As luck would have it Tony tells me we are going to meet on a specific day once a week. Well I didn't want to go because in my heart I am not ready; Tony had gone and had told me you should come. I really prayed about it and asked the Lord that if I was to make a commitment but did not go all the time to please be patient with me and that whatever group of people I was to be with would understand me.

Once again God answered my prayer in Charlie, Luella, Greg, Judy, Maxine, Rudy, Alex, Jubilee, Julie, Lou, David and Dolores. When we enter the home of our host and friend Charlie and Luella we are so welcomed with open arms, there is so much warmth and love when we are all together for we are truly a family of God, and we will all walk this pathway together as we search His word and wait for his Second Coming.

As long as I could remember growing up, my Mother would say, Noe when you see men running to and fro and knowledge increasing you will know the end is near. We live in a world where people are so busy with everything, that they do not take the time out with their one on one relationship with God. Every place you turn now, knowledge has increased so much that the time of the end is near. Am I afraid? I am only afraid if I am not ready for Gods return. As a child I use to sing this song, I want to be ready when Jesus comes, I didn't truly understand what I was singing now I do.

God has the power to change lives today no matter what the situation. If you ask Him in earnest, He will receive you. For me so many times I prayed and prayed and still He did not answer. I like so many others gave up so many times not believing that there is a God, a loving God. But I held on and my prayers were answered. I truly believe my story is a modern day miracle. God had to make me be part of that miracle because He saw me hanging on. My future is in Gods hand and I am excited to see in what direction He will take me.

To those who read this book, there is only one God, one Healer and all you have to do is reach out. He will stretch forth His hand if you have faith; just a simple act of faith. We are Gods children, we are His little lambs and he is the good Shepherd.

May God bless your reading of this book and may it help you find your way to the Masters Hand.

"And behold, I am coming quickly, and my reward is with me, to give to every one according to his work. "I am the Alpha and the Omega, *the* Beginning and *the* End, the First and the Last." Revelation 22:12-13